978473

G.

...STS.

10 FEB 1990

2 0 APR 2000

D1587171

COUNTY
RESERVE STOCK

2 0 DEC 2000

2 4 FEB 2005

L 33

Please renew/return this item by the last date shown.

So that your telephone call is charged at local rate, please call the numbers as set out below:

	From Area codes 01923 or 0208:	From the rest of Herts:
Renewals:	01923 471373	01438 737373
Enquiries:	01923 471333	01438 737333
Minicom:	01923 471599	01438 737599

L32b

EIGHT HUMORISTS

Eight Humorists

by

GEORGE MIKES

with drawings by David Langdon

LONDON

ALLAN WINGATE

First published in 1954 by
ALLAN WINGATE (*Publishers*) LTD.
12 *Beauchamp Place, London, S.W.*3.

Printed in the Channel Islands at the
Five Oaks Press, Jersey

All rights reserved

B54   4687

HERTFORDSHIRE
COUNTY LIBRARY
827·009
4
978773

CONTENTS

No! I am not Prince Hamlet, nor was meant to be;
Am an attendant lord, one that will do
To swell a progress, start a scene or two,
Advise the prince; no doubt, an easy tool,
Deferential, glad to be of use,
Politic, cautious, and meticulous;
Full of high sentence, but a bit obtuse;
At times, indeed, almost ridiculous—
Almost, at times, the Fool.

T. S. ELIOT
(The Love Song of J. Alfred Prufrock)

ON HUMOUR AND HUMORISTS

THE humorist may be, to some limited extent, the pet of readers but he is the step-child of critics. Newspaper reviewers do not mind occasionally dealing with a number of humorous books under such headlines as "A Bunch of Comics" or "Funny Ha-ha" and, more often than not, quote a humorist without quotation marks. Serious critics, however, neglect humorists to an alarming extent. About the humorists discussed in this book (with the exception of Mr. Evelyn Waugh), I could find hardly any serious essays and appreciations at all. In Mr. Edmund Wilson's two volumes, "The Shores of Light" and "Classics and Commercials"—being the literary chronicles of the twenties and thirties—James Thurber is not even mentioned and there is only one passing reference to Stephen Leacock. In the Columbia Encyclopaedia (pre-war edition) there is no entry under "humour".

To be a living writer is a great disadvantage in any case. To be a living humorist is a double disadvantage. I do not mean to suggest that from now on Shakespeare and Milton should be neglected and A. P. Herbert should take their place. The great heritage of literature must, of course, be kept alive; it is always possible to throw new light on even the most frequently discussed writer; and as the giants of bygone ages have an ever new meaning for each generation, it is right that they should be appraised afresh. But the essayists who have something new to say on Shakespeare and Milton are few and far between; yet books written about them are more than plentiful. A large number, indeed the majority, of these books are not written for the sake of the great man of the past but for the sake of the latest contributor. Ambition has taken various forms throughout the ages. At one time it was power most people wanted; at other times, money; at other times again social status; today the dominating driving power is snobbery, the "desire to belong". Intellectual snobbery is no better than any other kind. Many essayists feel that, being critics of Shakespeare, Milton or Dante they are being lifted up to a higher intellectual plane; while writing seriously about, say, James Thurber, they themselves would have to do the job of lifting. It is more pleasant to be lifted than to lift.

If the present book on contemporary humorists had been written by almost anybody else, I should welcome it with enthusiasm. As it is written by myself, I regard it with grave suspicion. I am unable to acquit myself of the very same charge of intellectual snobbism I have just been castigating. Only in me it works the other way round. My intention may have been as subconscious as an intention can be, but I have detected my secret and revealed my dishonest motive. By trying to write a book of serious essays about humorists and thus—at least as far as appearances are concerned—giving them the treatment usually allotted to more serious writers, I have tried to do a service to my own literary class and—if I may say so—first of all to myself. The fact that I have included myself in jocular fashion in the title, as the eighth of the outstanding humorous writers, is the final piece of evidence against myself. I hope the reader will not fall for such a transparent trick. (And will mistrust all moralists.)

*   *   *

The fact remains, however, that humorous authors are not treated fairly; and the reason for this unfairness can be traced back to a psychological attitude in critics and essayists.

The critics' crime is threefold. First, they do not take humorous writers seriously; second, they write both too little and too much about them; third, they try, very often successfully, to infuse a feeling of inferiority into them.

Taking the second point first, the most superficial research will convince anyone that humorists are either not mentioned at all, or else overpraised in a ridiculous and utterly uncritical manner. Their fate is either to suffer contemptuous silence or hardly less contemptuous superlatives. I have quoted in the chapter on Mr. P. G. Wodehouse two reviewers. One of them declared that his admiration for Wodehouse could hardly be described as "this side of idolatry"; the other, that a short piece by Wodehouse places him next to Homer, Dante and Shakespeare. On the other hand, as you can see in the chapter on Li'l Abner, Mr. John Steinbeck suggests that Mr. Al Capp, the creator of a comic strip, should be awarded the Nobel prize. I could quote similar wild exaggerations about all our eight humorists. Silence means dignified contempt; overpraise is a patronizing pat on the back.

What is then a true appraisal of the humorist? It is a stupid question but one that is bound to be raised. Naturally, his being a humorist does not place him in any value-category any more than his being a novelist or dramatist would. Tolstoy was a novelist; so is every hack who writes Westerns of a certain length. Why should Dickens and Mark Twain have more in common with the compiler of a volume called "A Good Joke for Every Occasion" than Molière with the author of the 1947 version of a pantomime on "Mother Goose"? A humorist is a writer, like the rest. He may make superficial fun on manners, he may crack jokes on the obvious or again he may be a serious and profound critic of society. He is liable to fail on two levels—as a writer and as a humorist—but once he has surmounted all these difficulties, he is worth notice. Yet, unless he can be idolised, he is rarely noticed at all.

It is the generally accepted idea that the humorist, ipso facto, belongs to a lower order of writers. There may be a grain of truth in this. A humorist, even at his best, has a limited appeal only. Tears may be reckoned superior to laughter since tears cleanse us while laughter makes us feel guilty. Euripides appeals to wider emotions and probably achieves deeper and more lasting effects than Aristophanes. Great tragedy is more emotional, and consequently less intellectual, than great humour. But being intellectual has not the supreme absolute value our age is inclined to attribute to it; *katharsis*, in Aristotle's sense of the word, remains the supreme achievement of literature. The greatest tragic writer is superior to the greatest humorist; Euripides is superior to Aristophanes; Tolstoy to Dickens; and *Hamlet* to the *Taming of the Shrew*. To a great extent we, humorists, need not have an inferiority complex; we are just inferior.

But Booth Tarkington is not superior to Jonathan Swift. And yet it is exactly this absurdity which is involved in the attitude which looks down upon humorists as lightweights simply because they try to achieve their effect by humorous means. This attitude does a great deal of harm because humorous writers tend to believe it, too. Most of them try to become more serious, not by saying something more serious in their own manner, but by saying something in a more serious manner. James Thurber has become more and more serious with the passing years—almost since his first book Evelyn Waugh has been growing gloomier, and possibly regards it now as an insult to be classified as a humorist; Charles Chaplin refuses to remain the greatest clown who ever lived and aspires to the rank of sixth-rate philospher; Stephen Leacock, although he thought more of himself as a humorist than as a scientist, also got quite near to plain, serious writing in his last book. It is Mr. Wodehouse alone who started in a certain vein and never apologised, never faltered, never changed.

Modern thought strongly rejects the close connection between the sublime and the ridiculous. Napoleon may have been right in saying that "it is only one step from the sublime to the ridiculous". He failed to add that from the ridiculous to the sublime is a very long mile.

*　　　　*　　　　*

What is humour? I don't know. I shall later on try to explain in greater detail how little I—and, I fear, all others —know about humour. Here it will suffice to say that essentially—at least for me—it is no less and no more than the original Latin word denotes: flavour. It is simply a special flavour, a way of looking at things.

Now a special flavour may tell us much about a certain thing, but surely it cannot tell enough. Let us take a flavour, for example: sweetness. If we know that something is sweet, we know it is not bitter or sour; we presume that we —or most of us—will like it. But still we have no idea what it is. Coffee may be sweet, tea may be sweet, a cake may be sweet and pineapple may be sweet. And precious little our knowledge about a substance is if we don't even know whether it is coffee, tea, cake, pineapple or something else. And even my distinction between sweet and sour is not exact. Something may be bitter and sweet or sour and sweet at the same time. Or else, we may like sweet things in general and still dislike a certain kind of sweet food in particular. I like almost everything sweet; but I could not eat a sweet salad.

My vague statement about humour—that it is a kind of flavour—does not tell us very much either. Nowadays, a sense of humour is regarded very highly. One of the gravest insults you can throw at a man is to say that he has no sense of humour. The reason for this is not the fact that not being able to understand a certain joke is worse than not being able to understand a serious train of thought. (Anyone would admit the latter but firmly deny the former.) The reason for our insistence on having an exquisite sense of humour cuts deeper. A sense of humour is considered the flower of a noble soul. The man with a sense of humour is supposed to have a sense of proportion; he is supposed to be able to look at things with detachment and see the smallness in the great and the ludicrous in the magnificent. He is able to laugh at himself—and this is regarded as one of the supreme human qualities. Perhaps I may be forgiven for quoting myself, instead of just repeating myself: ". . . a sense of humour may be a good or bad characteristic. A person who is too ironical—however witty he may be—is often a coward. He knows that he is a constant loser on the so-called battlefields of life and tries to console himself by laughing at love and beauty. That is why the Anglo-Saxons are so right in distrusting irony. Irony, on some occasions, may be an effective and justified weapon in the fight against wickedness, selfishness and stupidity; but in other cases it may only be the parting arrow of an inferior warrior, with which he tries to assert his non-existent superiority. Even the admirable ability to laugh at ourselves is often nothing else but inverted conceit. You are right in enjoying a good sense of humour; but be careful in admiring it." Yes, sarcasm may be a weapon to deflate the stupid and the pompous; but it may also be a weapon to bring the truly great down to our own inferior level. A sense of humour may be a sense of proportion; or else the complete lack of it. It may be the flower of a balanced nature and a wise general outlook but it may equally easily spring from bitterness, frustration, hatred and cowardice.

What follows from all this for the literary critic? Simply, that a humorist—quite apart from his value, quite apart from the question whether he is a good humorist or not—does not place himself in a closely definable caste just by being a humorist. Stephen Leacock saw the phoney and grotesque in pomposity and sham goodness; Mr. Punch sees the phoney and grotesque in the phoney and grotesque;

Mr. Thurber is annoyed and angered by humanity and consequently loves all human beings; Mr. Waugh is annoyed and angered by humanity and has consequently developed strong misanthropic tendencies; Mr. Chaplin seeks the grim Absolute, Mr. Wodehouse sticks to the gay Particular.

Humorists may be as manifold in their character as novelists or poets. If they are worthy of being judged at all, they should be judged as writers and only incidentally as humorists. This is so obvious a rule that I am almost ashamed to put it down; but it is so obvious a rule that hardly anybody follows it.

*   *   *

The one common characteristic shared by humorists is that they make us laugh—provided of course that they do. Some theatres and radio and television organisations measure the success of a comic show by registering the intensity of laughter by some electrical device. There was an age—alas, it has not yet passed—when the police was regarded as the highest authority in literary taste; it is almost natural that today electrical devices should take the place of the police. It was bound to happen in an age in which our love-life is being reduced to the level of Mr. Kinsey's statistics.

If you are tickled with a straw you are bound to laugh; if a comedian loses his trousers, people will laugh louder than at Max Beerbohm's wittiest *aperçues*. You can laugh with your belly and still be utterly bored; you may only smile with your eyes and be supremely entertained. The teeth are not the heart; nor are they the brain. The loudness of the laughter is no safer guide to a humorist's true value than is the noise of the battle to a general's strategical ability.

Why do people like to laugh? Laughter is always suspicious. It may be "sudden glory" indeed—but to feel glorious is not one of our highest aspirations. Or we may acquire a sudden surplus of physical energy—as Freud explained—which we then release in laughter. But again, to get rid of a burden is no real happiness. Crying should make us feel much better, because it purifies us. The Old Testament says: "Even in laughter the heart is sorrowful; and the end of mirth is heaviness."

But here the Old Testament is superficial. We are grateful to the man who makes us laugh. Laughter is a conspiracy. We always laugh at somebody's expense, even if that somebody is ourselves. Tears purify, laughter makes us feel guilty. That is exactly why we prefer laughter to tears. If someone makes us laugh, we share our guilt with him; if someone makes us cry, he makes us aware of his superiority. So we love laughter and dislike tears because we always prefer an accomplice to a preacher. We all prefer sudden glory to lasting purity. I do, at least.

*　　　*　　　*

And now I should like to return to the question: what is humour?

Well, what is rain? It is something different for the meteorologist and the farmer; for the bank clerk it may be the phenomenon which spoils his week-end, for the cinema-owner it may be the phenomenon which makes *his* week-end profitable. And are a drizzle and a downpour, a shower, a cloudburst and a drop here and there all rain? Is the difference between a drizzle and a deluge only a difference in degree or does it amount to a difference in kind? One can maintain that the difference is only one of degree—although one can hardly expect the ill-doers of antiquity who perished in the Deluge, to agree. One can also say that whatever different angles different individuals may have, rain is still rain, and scientific definition will lead to precise results.

But this is not true. There is nothing magic about science and in particular nothing magic about the methods which claim to be scientific. Different sciences may reach different results, even when dealing with the very same case. Legal insanity, for example, is vastly different from medical insanity. Physicians may diagnose a man sick; judges may call him a criminal. Medically he may be an invalid; but legally he will be hanged.

Similarly, the first difficulty in the definition of humour was that people approached it from different angles. Aristotle looked at it from an aesthetic point of view, Bergson as a philosopher and Freud as a psychologist. It is the story of rain, all over again.

I could summarise here all the leading theories but I shall not do so. They have been summarised often enough in excellent treatises. (See, for instance, F. L. Lucas: *Literature and Psychology*.) Nor will I go into the various classifications; the distinction between humour and wit; or into the categories of comedy, wit, joke, satire, irony, mimicry—the last subdivided into caricature, parody and travesty. There are also enlightening classifications. They do everything except answer the basic question: what is humour?

You may know many things about humour; you may use it with deadly or uproarious effect; you may enjoy it or earn your bread with it; you may classify it and discover penetrating truths about it. But you still do not know what it is. Similarly, physicists can produce electricity; they know all about it; with its help they can travel in the air, on land or on the water; they can dig tunnels, remove mountains, transmit messages thousands of miles, lighten our darkness and cure the sick with it: but they don't know what electricity is.

Of course, the problem of humour is not a literary but a philosophical question. Philosophy—if it is indeed a science—is the king of all sciences; philosophers have taught us all the wisdom about everything under the sun; they have raised a mighty monument of human knowledge but they have not yet solved even the very first question

B

they posed themselves thousands of years ago. In fact, they have never solved anything. Whenever they have succeeded in proving anything, other philosophers have equally convincingly proved its opposite. They have not solved the meaning of the universe and the aim of life; nor have they solved the question: what is humour. This last failure is more aggravating than the others. I, for one, am not certain at all that the universe has meaning and that life has an aim; but there *is* humour.

My own answer to the question "What is humour?" is, as I have already said, "I don't know." The answers given by Aristotle, Bergson and Freud (to mention just a few of those who have tried to give an answer) were incomparably better worded, more brilliantly expressed and more wittily developed than mine but they are essentially the same. Let's leave it at that. We don't need to know what humour is—in the proper philosophical sense—to go on enjoying humour. Just as we do not have to know what life is to go on living. "It is no part of the design of this treatise,"—wrote John Stuart Mill—"to aim at metaphysical nicety of definition where the ideas suggested by a term are already as determinate as practical purposes require."

*   *   *

My choice of humorists was haphazard. I do not claim that my humorists are the best; nor even that I like them all better than others not mentioned here. In fact, I hesitated a great deal before selecting one and omitting another.

For some time I thought of including Frederic Karinthy, an outstanding Hungarian humorist of great originality. He was a man who consciously suffered for not writing in English. He wanted to speak to the world—he felt—and not only to a parochial section of it. His work is practically unknown in this country, except for his "Journey Round My Skull" (published before the outbreak of the war)—a terrifying and moving description of brain operations, examined coolly and objectively, as if he were not himself the sufferer. This is an excellent piece of writing but not really characteristic of Karinthy in general. I had to leave him out on reflection; sad as it is for me, I do not think he would interest the British reader.

I also wanted to include Damon Runyon and Max Beerbohm. Runyon, with all his vulgarity and monotony, is the only poet in the lot: the poet of the metropolis. His work is the folklore of Broadway. Beerbohm again, with all his charm, wit, urbanity and the engaging twinkle in his eye, is—I feel—overvalued. He is good but he is not great. The very opposite of Meredith who is great but not good.

My only explanation for choosing my eight humorists in the way I have done is that there had to be eight of them and I have chosen these seven.

I

CHARLES CHAPLIN

DAVID LANGDON

S LOWLY it is being forgotten that Mr. Charles Chaplin is an artist. He has become as controversial a political figure as, for example, Mao Tse-Tung. You are either for or against Chaplin—it's either *homoousion* or *homoiousion*. If you are for him, you must accept *M. Verdoux* as a great film; if you are against him, you must reject even *The Gold Rush* as an insignificant piece of clowning. Because of his political views, he has been assailed on all levels and from all angles: political, artistic and even moral. And—again because of his political views—he has been acclaimed, by the other side, not only as a great clown but as a great thinker, philanthropist and hero. This is all the more surprising since Mr. Chaplin has no political views worth speaking of.

First of all, instead of having political ideas, he is merely possessed by certain emotions which may be relevant also on a political plane. He instinctively sides with the underdog and revolts against authority and dignity. However generous these feelings may be they certainly do not constitute a political philosophy. Artistically he is a split personality (I shall have a great deal more to say on this presently) and he has succeeded in splitting the personality of many Americans; indeed, not only splitting into two—but splitting into psychological atoms. His love for the underdog was accepted by Americans because they are nice and emotional people who like siding with the weak; but it was, at the same time, angrily rejected, because America is the country of the overdogs. American society is a society of climbers—not in the derogatory sense of the word, it is simply a society where practically everyone is actively engaged in reaching a higher social and financial status—and the American climber never looks at the summit, which is practically unattainable, but looks back at his starting point. The more people below him, the higher he must have climbed. It is the optimism of the man in the queue who keeps looking back to see how many people are behind him. This outlook is not the result of an insatiable power complex; it is simply a way of measuring things. Then again the Americans are all one with Chaplin in his revolt against authority and all against him in his contempt for dignity. Their revolt against authority is not anarchistic—it is purely personal. They approve of authority in principle; they approve of authority over the other fellow and over obnoxious and subversive groups—but not over themselves. On the individual plane, the challenge to authority—never the defiance of it—is the symbol of freedom. Chaplin's defiance of authority has a strong anarchist element in it—so even this part of his character, while it may be accepted, is always regarded with suspicion. His ridicule of dignity is again definitely disliked. The American hankers after dignity but has resigned himself to the fact that, whatever he may become, dignified he will never be. The American will loudly protest that his informality is a virtue and the right to sit in his shirtsleeves, wear a hat in the house and put his feet on the table amounts to a creed with him; but if he hates the British for one thing, it is for the Briton's dignity. He tries to laugh at it and although British dignity *is* often ridiculous, the American laughs with the wrong side of his mouth. (If he hates the British for *two* things, the second is that the Briton is not a climber; he is content where he is—almost content even if he comes a cropper in general or individual misfortune.) The American looks at Chaplin with suspicion: isn't Charlie after all a caricature of him-self? The tramp who dines with millionaires one day and has not enough to eat the next? The dignified underdog who despises dignity and is always kicked in the pants? The adventurer who depends too much on luck? Of course, Chaplin never intended to caricature the Americans in such an unfair way. The differences between Charlie and a caricature of the average American are much greater than the similarities. The United States happened to provide the sites for his films but his personality was formed in the East End of London. But whatever the picture intended, it is disturbing.

Mr. Chaplin—the subject of violent political contro-versy—has, in fact, never expressed any political ideas. As far as one can make out from his films, he is not a socialist, he is not a Communist; by political standards he is not even on the Left. His tramp does not represent any politic-ally important class—after all, tramps do not aspire to political power—and he has never attacked capitalists. Is then the great emotional—and essentially political—hubbub around him unjustified? Of course it isn't. The truth is that he is much more dangerous than any Socialist plus Communist rolled into one. He is an anarchist—certainly not a confessed, probably even not a conscious anarchist—but an anarchist all the same. He has never attacked capital-ism but he has often shown that our whole social order is stupid, wicked and even criminal; that tramps are worthier people than the successful climbers and murderers more honest than society at large; that this society is not even worthy of a real fight; it should be held in contempt and laughed at. This teaching is the basis of his unpopularity in America and his popularity over here. Britain—and the whole of Europe—is old and settled down; a little disruption would be good for Britain and Europe; but American society is not cohesive enough, it is nervous and just cannot take Chaplin's anarchistic humour calmly. Accordingly it is either accepted with passionate eagerness or rejected with horrified hatred.

*　　　　*　　　　*

Chaplin has now sided with his enemies. He has given in to them and pulled the flags down. His own battle is being waged on different battlefields—but he was quite pleased to accept temporary defeat which, he thought, meant victory for him. He left America and silenced Charlie.

Because Charlie, the tramp, is the real villain in Mr. Chaplin's life. Chaplin created Charlie; and Charlie created Chaplin. Charlie was the world-famous figure—with his own character, own personality and even his own external appearance. The world was taken by Charlie—perhaps Walt Disney's creatures were the only other comic creations which took the world by almost equally violent storm— and it was only because the natural constitution of things demanded it, that the world decided there had to be a real personality behind Charlie. But the world cared precious little for Mr. Chaplin—it only loved Charlie with a warm, passionate and possessive love. The Charlie versus Chaplin relationship is a complicated and important one. It caused happiness, then a strain, followed by tension; it has led to jealousy and ultimately to attempted murder. Mr. Chaplin tried to kill Charlie, and the motive was exasperation and revenge. But to understand the whole story we must begin at the beginning.

*　　　　*　　　　*

I shall not attempt to draw a full portrait of Mr. Charles Chaplin. A whole library has been written about him—the two last volumes to appear here being *The Little Fellow* by Peter Cotes and Thelma Miklaus (Bodley Head) and *The Great Charlie* by Robert Payne (Deutsch). Neither of these is really good; both are useful, informative and conscientious. In common with the whole Chaplin literature—indeed, in common with almost the entire range of literature concerned with comic artists—they are adulatory and not critical. I shall not try to fill the gap—even if I were capable of doing so—I am mainly concerned here with the Charlie-Chaplin relationship.

*   *   *

The year 1889 was an important one in the history of the cinema. In that year Edison invented the Kinetoscope in the United States and, in England, Charles Spencer Chaplin was born. Chaplin's father—Charles Chaplin senior —was a well-known music-hall singer and his mother, Hannah, was also a small-time artist and singer, appearing under the name of Lily Harley. Charles, junior, spent his babyhood—with his elder half-brother, Sidney—touring the provincial stages in a bassinet. Chaplin was still a small child when his father died in London's St. Thomas's Hospital. Years of almost inhuman misery—and superhuman happiness followed. Chaplin watched his mother sacrifice her job, her career and her health for the children's sake. She could take no stage-engagements. The children, dressed in rags, wandered about hungrily in the streets of South London. Charlie sold newspapers at Ludgate Circus. Sidney and Charles made toys out of cardboard, wastepaper and matchsticks and tried to sell them to more fortunate children. And—quoting from *The Little Fellow* —"Charlie was already showing an unusual gift for dancing and one of their favourite ways of earning money was to follow a barrel-organ man until he reached a pitch. Then Charlie would dance and attract an amused crowd; while Sidney took round the hat. Quick as lightning the children would run off with the money taken, pursued by the cries of the organ-grinder who suddenly realized he was to have no share in the profits."

The whole future pattern is already discernible from

this small incident. Charlie's love for the streets; his rebellion against the established order; his dancing, and even Sidney's taking the hat round. (Sidney—following up these early beginnings—later became managing director of the Chaplin film company.) But the significance of these incidents is even deeper: it was then and there that Chaplin became convinced of the basic injustice of our social order. It was unjust that stealing was the only way he could make money. It was not he who was the thief, but society itself which first withheld his due and later compelled him to steal. The lifelong struggle between Charlie the tramp and the police really started there, in the streets of South London—Charlie always being the hero and the police the villains. And, to make matters worse, Chaplin, in spite of everything, was very happy in this life. Mr. Somerset Maugham writes: " . . . he suffers from a nostalgia of the slums. The celebrity he enjoys, his wealth, imprison him in a way of life in which he finds only constraint. To him the streets of Southern London are the scene of frolic, gaiety and extravagant adventure."

Chaplin, at the age of 18, became a member of Fred Karno's company. Karno was one of the important theatrical figures of the time and later he described Chaplin in these words: "He wasn't very likeable. I've known him go whole weeks without saying a word to anyone in the company. Occasionally he would be quite chatty, but on the whole he was dour and unsociable. He lived like a monk . . ." When he received his first leading part in a comedy called "Jimmy the Fearless" he showed so little enthusiasm or even interest that the part was taken away from him and given to a man called Stanley Jefferson. Stanley Jefferson later became Stan Laurel of the Laurel and Hardy duo.

In the early days of the film, Chaplin went to America and was eventually attracted by the new medium. From that time it was plain sailing for him—as far as outward success was concerned. Let me quote some of the inevitable figures. In his first year in American films—1914—he made 35 films—some in a few days and others in a few hours. His first contract secured him 125 dollars a week—nearly three times as much as he received from Karno. Soon he was offered 1000 dollars a week but he asked for 1075. This was an odd figure, and he had to explain: "I need the extra 75 dollars to live on. The 1000 dollars I wish to save up." The boy from the Kennington slums who had felt the pangs of hunger just could not believe that his fabulous luck would last. Not long afterwards, a new company offered him 5000 dollars a week which—on the advice of his brother Sidney—he rejected to accept 10,000 dollars instead—the largest sum paid to any film-star up to that time. He also received a bonus of 150,000 dollars in one lump sum. He was well under 30. When he came to London in the early twenties—he was and still is a British subject—he received 73,000 letters in three days. He discovered with some astonishment that he had 700 relatives in London. Nine of them claimed to be his mother.

This is the life story we learn from the two books mentioned. But the life of Charlie—Chaplin's immortal tramp —is of even more interest and importance.

There are three distinct phases in Charlie's career. The bowler hat, the moustache, the cane, the huge boots and the white carnation in the buttonhole were there from the outset. (The moustache was the symbol of vanity; the cane the symbol of dignity; and he borrowed the boots from a Kennington cabman he had known well.) The acrobatic skill, the dance, the mime and the slapdash were the natural gifts which made him celebrated. His war on society was declared in his first films. He was chased by innumerable policemen and even when he, himself, became a policeman in "Easy Street", he was helping poor women to steal vegetables and potatoes. Sometimes brutal, he was yet unfailingly kind to the poor and helpless; he was hungry for love; he was terribly lonely and although he was—as becomes the "little man"—a constant loser on all battlefields, he accepted his lot, not with dignity, but with supreme indifference.

Then came the second phase. Charlie, already famous, became truly great. What he expressed in mime, in dance and in slapdash comedy, took on a universal significance. The tramp who cooked and ate his shoes in the *Gold Rush* —consuming shoelaces as if they were macaroni and breaking a nail as if it were a wishbone—remains an eternal picture of human forlornness and wretchedness; a symbol of futility and amiable snobbishness. There he was, the little man in the big world, always defeated yet always victorious, always crushed but indestructible, unloved but adorable, more comic than anything else in the world we had known before but also sadder, more moving and more pathetic. He was unbearably sentimental sometimes but one forgave him just as one forgave Dickens. In his later short films but especially in *The Kid*, *The Gold Rush*, *Circus*, *City Lights* and *Modern Times* he shone as no clown had ever shone before.

By that time, the relationship between Chaplin and Charlie had become a very complicated one. First, Chaplin loved Charlie, was grateful to him and, not unnaturally, identified himself with him. Charlie not only brought fame, success and a fortune to Mr. Chaplin but also meant the realisation of his dreams and the perfect expression of his personality. He was himself the lovable tramp, the inglorious crusader, the fearless knight in shiny trousers.

For long the relationship of Chaplin and Charlie was ideal. In time, perhaps they ceased to exist as an identical person and lived happily and peacefully side by side: the soft-spoken, white-haired millionaire and the unkempt, ragged tramp; the company director and employer of a huge staff, and the rebellious anarchist; the little sad-hearted success and the world's most successful failure.

Then the change came. Slowly it dawned on Mr. Chaplin that he was not the real man of the two; Charlie was the genuine one. Chaplin used to be free and happy in the slums—and had become a prisoner in his new life. Charlie was still free and happy—Chaplin was not. Slowly he grew more and more bitter. Charlie had stolen the limelight from him and become his prison-warder. Nobody took any interest in Chaplin; he was lonelier and more forgotten than in the London Slums: it was Charlie who was victorious. Nobody spoke of "Mr. Chaplin"—people talked of Charlie. Or just look at the titles of the two books I have mentioned: one is called *The Great Charlie*, the other *The Little Fellow*. Chaplin could talk to millions but only in Charlie's voice; Charlie determined for him what he could say and how he could say it. He did not even possess a face of his own; it was Charlie's face that looked at the world with pathetic sadness.

Slowly Chaplin grew jealous of Charlie. At first there was no violence. Chaplin simply and modestly tried to re-assert his own personality. He was no actor—he was a brilliant mimic and an even more brilliant clown—but he wanted to act; and he wanted to put in a few words of his own here and there. People listened politely—with some embarrassment—but quite patiently, too, because they knew that sooner or later Chaplin would give way to Charlie again. Here I quote a short passage from the final speech in *The Great Dictator*.

"Soldiers, don't give yourselves to brutes, men who despise you and enslave you, regiment your lives, tell you what to do, what to think and what to feel, who drill you, diet you, treat you like cattle, use you as cannon fodder. Don't give yourself to these unnatural men—machine men with machine minds and machine hearts. You are not machines. You are not cattle. You are men. You have the

c

love of humanity in your hearts, you don't hate. Only the unloved hate—the unloved and the unnatural. Soldiers, don't fight for slavery, fight for liberty."

Has anybody read in print anything sillier, flatter and more artless? How different was the great dictator's dance with the globe which in the end he embraced with such a passion that it exploded. That dance was a creation of a genius; the speech about love, humanity and peace was a disheartening collection of pompous clichés and bombastic platitudes. Chaplin felt it; we all knew it; and Charlie giggled. So Chaplin in a fit of fury and jealousy made an attempt on Charlie's life. He believes that he has killed it —but he is wrong. This attempted murder opens up the third phase in Charlie's career. At the moment he is a ghost.

Mr. Chaplin was not content to be the clown of genius; he decided to become a writer and thinker of the first order. He thought that the way to his new greatness was to say in plain words badly what Charlie had said in mime, gesture and dance superbly well. He wanted to say more than before, but said alas, considerably less.

"Poetry is more valuable than cricket,"—wrote the late Professor G. H. Hardy*—"but Bradman would be a fool if he sacrificed his cricket in order to write second-rate minor poetry." These are words Mr. Chaplin ought to have pondered over.

It was in *Monsieur Verdoux* that he first said *expressis verbis* what he had expressed many times before: that our society was a society of criminals and that even the professional murderer was often a man of gentle feelings compared with some honest citizen. According to Clausewitz war is the logical extension of diplomacy; according to Chaplin murder is the logical extension of social life. All that was told too crudely; in the way it was expressed, it sounded silly; and reiterated with the solemn pomposity of

*A Mathematician's Apology, Cambridge University Press

Verdoux, instead of the impish gloom of Charlie, we realised that it all had been said a million times before. On top of this, Charlie was a brilliant and original talent; Verdoux was a provincial ham.

Limelight was much better. The story takes place in London, in 1914. It is a story of fear—the fear felt by a young ballerina who is terrified of facing her audience. To avoid the ordeals of success or failure she attempts suicide. She is saved by an old music-hall artist who was, once upon a time, the rage of London but is now going to the dogs because he drinks too much. And he drinks too much because he is terified himself. The old artist inspires the girl and gives her her courage back, but he cannot cure himself and on the evening of his triumphant come-back, he dies on the stage watching the beautiful young ballerina dance. All this could be very good but as it is, it is merely acceptable. Yet the film is a great and memorable film—because Charlie's ghost appears in it, too. The ghost—resembling in appearance the deceased—performs an act as a flea-trainer and later as a violinist (in which latter scene another great clown, Mr. Buster Keaton is his partner) and it must be quite clear to any spectator that Charlie's ghost is more triumphantly alive than the old music-hall artist, his young ballerina or any other member of the caste. At one point Chaplin picks a rose, smells it, sighs—then puts a little sugar on it and eats it. This scene is more memorable and, if you like, more profound than all his second-hand philosophising and pseudo-wisdom. Charlie's ghost was allowed to sneak back and he stole the show. He refused to lie low; he jumped out of his coffin and claimed his rights. Of course, no one can tell an artist—especially an artist of Mr. Chaplin's standing—what he *should* do; but one can tell him that one thing he does is superb and the other is worse than bad: it is mediocre.

The artist's jealousy of his own creation is not new. Conan Doyle, too, grew jealous of Sherlock Holmes and

Rodin of his statues. Doyle tried to kill Holmes but was compelled to resurrect him. Rodin realised later that there was no need for him to be jealous of his statues because he, Rodin, would live on in his work. So will Mr. Chaplin live in Charlie—who, after all, has no independent life. It is not only his creation: it is he, himself. He cannot kill Charlie without killing himself. Indeed, he can kill himself as an artist without harming Charlie at all. Mr. Chaplin must resign himself to never becoming a third-rate moralist and sixth-rate philosopher; he must be content—with a deep sigh—to remain the most ingenious of all clowns—the most serious, thought-provoking and uproarious, the saddest and most loveable clown who ever trod this globe.

THE FILMS OF MR. CHARLES CHAPLIN

1914:

Making a Living
Kid Auto Races at Venice
Mabel's Strange Predicament
Between Showers
A Film Johnnie
Tango Tangles
His Favourite Pastime
Cruel, Cruel Love
The Star Boarder
Mabel at the Wheel
Twenty Minutes of Love
Caught in a Cabaret
Caught in the Rain
A Busy Day
The Fatal Mallet
Her Friend the Bandit
The Knockout
Mabel's Busy Day
Mabel's Married Life

Laughing Gas
The Property Man
The Face on the Bar-room Floor
Recreation
The Masquerader
His New Profession
The Bounders
The New Janitor
Those Love Pangs
Dough and Dynamite
Gentlemen of Nerve
His Musical Career
His Trysting Place
Tillie's Puncture Romance (6 reels)
Getting Acquainted
His Prehistoric Past

1915:
His New Job
A Night Out
The Champion
The Jitney Elopement
The Tramp
By the Sea
Work
A Woman
The Bank
Shanghaied
A Night in the Show
Carmen (4 reels)
Police
Triple Trouble

1916:
The Floorwalker
The Fireman
The Vagabond

One A.M.
The Count
The Pawnshop
Behind the Screens
The Rink

1917:
Easy Street
The Cure
The Immigrant
The Adventurer

1918:
A Dog's Life (3 reels)
The Bond
Shoulder Arms (3 reels)

1919:
Sunnyside (3 reels)
A Day's Pleasure

1921:
The Kid (6 reels)
The Idle Class

1922:
Pay Day

1923:
The Pilgrim (4 reels)
A Woman of Paris (8 reels)

1925
The Gold Rush (9 reels)

1928:
The Circus (7 reels)

1931:
City Lights (87 minutes)

1936:
Modern Times (85 minutes)

1940:
  The Great Dictator (126 minutes)

1947:
  Monsieur Verdoux (125 minutes)

1952:
  Limelight (129 minutes)

NOTE: All these films, unless otherwise specified, were one
      or two reel shorts.

2

STEPHEN LEACOCK

STEPHEN LEACOCK was one of the most engaging split personalities of literary history. In contrast with the innumerable clowns who want to play Hamlet, he was the professor who wished to remain—indeed, to become —a clown. "There is no trouble," (he wrote) "in writing a scientific treatise on the folklore of Central China, or a statistical enquiry into the declining population of Prince Edward Island. But to write something out of one's own mind, worth reading for its own sake, is an arduous contrivance only to be achieved in fortunate moments, few and far between. Personally, I would sooner have written 'Alice in Wonderland' than the whole Encyclopaedia Britannica."

He thought it was his duty to take himself seriously but never quite managed to do so. He was not very much impressed by himself. Socially he did not rise. He came from a family of farmers—gentlemen farmers, at that—and these people, for one reason or another, always regard themselves as being on top of the social ladder. A worker, particularly if he considers himself a "proletarian", can rise easily; a barrister may become a Queen's Counsel; a small shopkeeper a captain of industry, and a Crown Prince a King. But for a gentleman farmer there is no possibility of advancement. He can only decline. And the Leacocks did decline. Then, he was born an Englishman and Englishmen cannot rise either. Leacock became a patriotic Canadian citizen but always remembered his higher origin. But his intellectual status was a different question. He loved McGill University and liked the idea of being a professor. He tried to be dignified; he tried to be jealous of his academic rank and scientific achievements. But whenever he was introduced to a distinguished and learned gathering—as the renowned professor and Doctor of seven Universities— Chicago, Queen's, McGill, Dartmouth, Brown, Toronto and Lennoxville—he would stand up and reprove the chairman; "You've forgotten that I'm also the President of the Anti-Mosquito Association of East Simcoe."

It was not his desire to convince the world that he was a humorist by trade but a Dostoevsky at heart; he made no attempt even to prove the opposite proposition that while he might be a dull economist by profession he was at the same time "the Mark Twain of the British Empire". He wanted to become the Stephen Leacock of the British Empire and in this, he succeeded. He had a high regard for his own literary work and was proud of being an excellent stylist; he even tried to become one of his own numerous admirers. In this he never succeeded.

He never tried consciously to spread wisdom in jocular form. He simply looked around in his own world with his own eyes and described things as he saw them. He did not look far and his gaze did not penetrate deeply. His world was the world of the University, of Orillia, the world of teaching and lecturing, reading books and fishing. Whenever he tried to look at wider horizons his vision became cloudy; whenever he tried to tackle larger problems his strength failed him. His description of Mr. Joshua Smith, the innkeeper at Mariposa, is a little masterpiece. He made Mr. Smith—for everybody else probably an ordinary, mildly amusing creature—a figure of first class fun. But, in turn, he turned Dickens into a literary Joshua Smith, one writer among many, repeating about him things which have been said many times before. He could say uproariously funny things about literary technique, about the habits, characteristics and behaviour of people, he recognized the oddities of every-day life but whenever he attempted to analyze the Empire, Canada, or even his own métier, humour, he became dull and platitudinous. He could not see what Central Europeans would call the Great Connection Between Things. This was his great failing in his serious and semi-serious writing and, at the same time, his shining virtue in his humorous works.

He found a formula because he never looked for one. It never entered his mind that a formula existed or was something to look for. His formula was that there was no formula, that life was confused, illogical and silly but very amusing and worth living. He discovered that life was life—and so few had noticed that before him. His laughter was not cynical, nor sophisticated; it was broad, loud and healthy. His light was not the penetrating but focussed and concentrated ray of a headlight; it was warming—if not dazzling—sunshine. He did not understand people but caught them in their psychological *negligée*. He could not analyze, but he could draw a caricature. He could not show us to ourselves—but he could show us up.

Leacock, the Anglo-Canadian, was a typical British genius. He loved order but never kept order. He laid down strict rules for himself, for his pupils and farm-hands but broke the rules whenever commonsense dictated this, or whenever he forgot all about his own rules. Fortune and misfortune he took alike in good humour. The scale of his reactions reached from the smile to the shrug of the shoulder. He was hospitable because he liked people and also because every guest was an excuse for a party. Preparatory to larger parties, he would calculate the expenses with an economist's skill and expert knowledge—and forget all about the results the next day. He bred turkeys and one Thanksgiving day he dined on the last survivor of a brood of one hundred. About his farming exploits, he wrote: "I have a large country house—a sort of farm which I carry on as a hobby . . . ten years ago the deficit on my farm was about a hundred dollars; but by well designed capital expenditure, by drainage and greater attention to detail, I have got it into the thousands." (That country house at Orillia was, of course, more than a hobby to him. It was a necessity. It was the real manifestation of his success. His father was ruined by farming and now Leacock wanted to prove to himself that he could keep a farm and afford to lose money on it. He proudly called Orillia "the House that Jokes built".)

No, he could not be pompous even if he tried. About a very successful lecture tour on Imperial Organization he said: "When I state that these lectures were followed almost immediately by the Union of South Africa, the Banana Riots in Trinidad, and the Turco-Italian war, I think the reader can form some opinion of their importance."

His attitude to the more important matters in life was equally sane. He became first a lecturer at McGill University and later Head of the Department of Economics and Political Science. As this position was one of the prizes of his profession, he regarded himself as singularly fortunate. "The emolument is so high," (he wrote) "as to place me distinctly above the policemen, postmen, street-car conductors, and other salaried officials of the neighbourhood, while I am able to mix with the poorer of the business men of the city on terms of something like equality." At the age of 65 he was forced to retire . . . "much against my will, on grounds of senility." When he reached his 70th birthday, he studied the old man in himself with bewildered amusement. He noticed that he had grown kinder in his judgment of others. The old man, he realized, was able to comprehend, if not to pardon, the sins and faults of his fellowmen. "If I hear of a man robbing a cash register of the shop where he works, I think I get the idea. He wanted the cash. If I read of a man burning down his store to get the insurance, I see that what he wanted was the insurance. He had nothing against the store. Yet somehow just when I am reflecting on my own kindliness, I find myself getting furious with a waiter for forgetting the Worcester Sauce." He faced death itself with the same equanimity. He was not afraid of it; on the other hand Bertrand Russell's cool contempt for old people who wish to live forever was also alien to him. He shrugged his shoulders once again. Death? Perhaps it was inevitable. And he died of cancer of the throat at the age of 75.

He was neither too frank, nor too brave. He wrote little about himself. There is a brief autobiographical preface to the *Sunshine Sketches of a Little Town*, a small number of short pieces about himself and finally his unfinished autobiography, *The Boy I Left Behind Me*. Though he never wanted to write his autobiography, he gave some material about himself to his niece and secretary, Mrs. Barbara Nimmo and asked her to write a book about him after his death. Then he had to spend a few months between two operations—a few quiet months—but he could not rest. He used the collected notes to write his last book and reached about half way through his life. The second operation followed and Leacock died shortly afterwards.

He was not a religious man but he never wrote against religion or about religion. This was, however, not cowardice. He was a fighter of small battles, not of big ones. "I had no real 'nerve', no real 'gall',"—he said quite rightly. The evasion of another subject—his anti-monarchist feelings— seems more opportunist. He declared that from the age of eight the theory of a republic, the theory of equality, and the condemnation of hereditary rights seemed obvious and self-evident truths to him. But he added: "I stopped short at the Queen," (meaning, of course, Queen Victoria). Why? Mostly because this question touches on ground "on which I didn't propose to tread". If this is not self-confessed evasion, what is? He said that for him a hereditary Lord

D

didn't have a leg to stand on. And later he spoke of . . .
"my underlying Jeffersonian republicanism: back I slip to
such crazy ideas that all men are equal, and that hereditary
rights (still leaving out the British monarch) are hereditary
wrongs." But surely, if you are a republican, you cannot
leave the monarch out of consideration. Still, I believe this
compromise did not spring from cowardice. He was a
revolutionary of a very mild brand—a revolutionary who
detested revolution. He was a revolutionary—or rather a
good natured gambler—on a household and club level. He
was a conservative and while rejecting the rights of a
hereditary class, he accepted the rights of a propertied class
and knew perfectly well that the two may stand or fall
together. But possibly, he did not even go as far as that. Put
simply, he was a republican who genuinely approved of the
monarchy.

As a humorist, Stephen Leacock relied on his sense of
nonsense (the one being a sub-division of the other) and
was greatly fortified by an excellent sense of parody. His
burlesque imitations of all the fashionable reading of his
time—romantic novels, Russian sentimental novels, detect-
ive novels, etc.—still make us cry with laughter, not only
because his descriptions are so funny in themselves, but also
because his observations are so painlessly true.

He discovered such basic and simple truths as: "All
boarding houses are the same boarding house." At the same
time he dared to be gloriously non-sensical. This was still
possible and welcome in an age more sure of itself than ours.
Quite a number of his titles refer to idiocy of one kind or
another: *Nonsense Novels, Frenzied Fiction, Moonbeams
from the Larger Lunacy, Further Foolishness*. His general
and basic technique was exaggeration. Where you expect
a sigh, he thunders; where you expect a slight shading, he
draws three thick lines in red and green; where you expect
a solitary, frightened figure, he brings in a regiment with a
brass band; where you expect a murmur, he fires a salvo

of twelve guns. He never used the engaging and disarming idiocy of Edward Lear. Instead of the absence and reversal of sense, he relied on such exaggeration as turned sense into nonsense—thus basically siding with sense and sobriety. If there is an atmosphere of secrecy around spies, there is such perfect secrecy around Leacock's spies that the spy himself does not know where he is. "A friend of mine . . . one of the most brilliant men in the Hungarian Secret Service, once spent a month in New York under the impression that he was in Winnipeg."

A spy, of course, must disguise himself. And disguise himself all the time. He—the spy takes a room in an hotel. "I was muffled up to avoid recognition, in a long overcoat with the collar turned up and reaching well above my ears, while the black beard and moustache, that I had slipped on in entering the hotel, concealed my face." Then, in Leacock's spy-stories everybody is a spy—as, indeed, for the spy everybody must be a spy. The ambulance-man who helped a friend who fainted in the street (having been terrified of a spy) was the famous Russian spy, Poulispantzoff. (He had met him only twice before. Once when they were both disguised as Zulus at Bulawayo and once in China, before Poulispantzoff made his entry into Tibet, concealed in a tea case.) Having seen Poulispantzoff, he was not surprised to read a few hours afterwards that the uncle of the young king of Siam had been assassinated. He could not, however, reveal the connection between these two events. The consequences to the Vatican would be too serious.

Canada, for the British traveller, always seems an odd mixture of things British and American. Leacock's humour is very Canadian in this sense, too. His spy's wild boasting seems to be of American origin, although it is, in fact, mock British modesty: "I shall always feel, to my regret, that I am personally responsible for the outbreak of the present war." His use of anti-climax is English: ". . . a single *faux pas* might prove a false step." But he often uses this anti-climax technique on such a gigantic American scale that the product must be labelled as Canadian: "I read in the newspapers that a German army has invaded France and was fighting the French, and that the English expeditionary force had crossed the Channel. 'This,'—I said to myself—'means war.' As usual, I was right."

His observations go deeper than mere parody of the spy-atmosphere and mentality of these novels. He makes fun of the spies and agents who keep talking of mortal dangers and live a life of princely luxury: "It was necessary for me to be here, there and everywhere, visiting all the best hotels, watering places, summer resorts, theatres, and places of amusement."

He was also aware of the snob-appeal of spy-stories, which is often stronger for the reader than the adventure-appeal. His spy is instructed to mix freely with members of the American cabinet. As far as the President of the United States was concerned, his spy was instructed to mix with him on a footing of the most open-handed friendliness. ("Footing of open-handed friendliness" was the kind of stylistic joke that few readers noticed but of which he was very fond.) The spy was told to be at the White House continually. He failed, however. He worked hard for five months—always willing to dine with the American cabinet —but they did not invite him. No invitation came from the British Embassy either, for an informal midnight supper with the Ambassador. Anyone who knows anything of the inside working of the international spy-system will realize that without these invitations one can do nothing. His spy, of course, was not discouraged by this temporary setback. He sent a note (needless to say, in cipher) to the President of the United States to tell him that "I am ready to dine with you on any day that may be convenient to both of us."

Sometimes he overworks a joke and rides it to death —where is the humorist who doesn't? He does it with silly jokes which were stillborn to start with, or overdone before cropping up in their present form. The spy's boss tells him:

"The United States, as you have perhaps heard, is making war against Germany."

Then, as if the "as you have perhaps heard" were not enough, he goes on:

"I have heard so,"—I replied.

And even then he goes on squeezing the last fluid ounce of humour out of it:

"Yes,"—continued Gestern. "The fact has leaked out."

And a last squeeze:

". . . how, we do not know."

A final twist is often used at the end of Leacock's stories. This twist is often of a financial character—on borrowing money, an allusion to the pennilessness of the hero or some fraud. The spy never pays his bills and is intent on touching everybody for some cash. Leacock's family went through very hard times and, no doubt, he was very proud of being able to pay his bills. This may be why jokes about money became quite an obsession with him. His spiritualist stories (some of them brilliant) are usually stories of fraud—which, I believe, may be forgiven in a humorist, if not in a spiritualist. But one could give almost endless other examples of this kind of solution. The prince, who grants an interview, steals the interviewer's fountain pen; the scientist, on the other hand, pays the journalist for the interview. A parody of a play—in *Behind the Beyond*, and an excellent one even by Leacock's very high standards—ends with these words: ". . . in the office, is a man in a circus waistcoat adding up dollars with a blue pencil, and he knows that the play is right." His amusing dentist-story, too, ends with a fantasy on the dentists' bill. Another piece—on meeting an old friend and having no idea who he may be—starts very well but is turned into a rather silly and vulgar story of fraud. So does the otherwise vastly entertaining piece of palm-reading. And so on and so on. I should add, however, that one of his earliest and best stories on his "financial career" also belongs to this category—the one where he describes how he put a small sum in a new bank-account and withdrew it immediately by mistake.

Many writers have shown us many times how superior intelligence can squash affectation and how a clever remark can deflate the senseless desire "to be different". It was Leacock who showed us how stupidity and lack of understanding can do this much better.

"I am going,"—I said—"to spend a month naked alone in the woods."

He (the young man's boss) looked up from his desk with genial kindness.

"That's right,"—he said, "get a good rest."

"My plan is,"—I added—"to live on berries and funguses."

"Fine,"—he answered.

University professors were one of his favourite targets. But he could never make up his mind about them. This was another aspect of his jovially and not very tragically split personality. He was proud of being a professor but at the same time ashamed of being proud of anything. Pride was no part of his nature. Probably this conflict is the explanation for another recurring motive in his writings. He liked to show us how stupid men instruct—very successfully —equally stupid ones in subjects they know nothing about. Take, for instance, the piece in which the High Authority explains the war situation. (War, by the way, in all these instances means World War I.) The explanation is extremely funny but the main point is that no one, including, of course, the High Authority himself, understands a word about anything. The audience nod, laugh, murmur and sigh with relief whenever required to do so. They are happy when they hear that there will be a Zollverein and an Ausgleich. They frown anxiously when the High

Authority declares that they may abolish the Cypriotic Suzerainty of the Porte. But when he adds: "These are matters of indifference,"—they all assume a look of utter indifference.

There was a vast difference in his eyes—as indeed, there is—between the various grades of teaching. Being a professor was one thing but being a teacher was another. He loathed the memory of his teaching days and thought that ordinary school-teaching was a miserable profession. His days at school—both as a pupil and as a teacher—remained very vivid in his memory and he wrote a great deal about teaching without, however, contributing many original ideas to pedagogy. It is interesting to note that he condemned the "funny teacher"—with some wise reservations: ". . . don't try to be funny; feeble teachers attempt a footing of fun as a means of getting together. The real teacher only descends to fun when he has established a sufficient height to descend from."

He knew that the best way to achieve selfish aims was to behave like an utterly unselfish philanthropist. Mr. Smith, (the hotel-keeper at Mariposa) asked the merry-go-round man what he charged for a ride. "Two for a nickel," said the man. "Take that,"—said Mr. Smith, handing out a ten-dollar bill from a roll of money—"and ride the little folks free all evening." He sold forty dollars worth of lager alone that night and Mr. Smith learned, if he had not already suspected it, the blessedness of giving.

Leacock was a moral and decent, even a conventional man, but he hated moralising. He wrote against work and raised his voice in praise of drinks and good food. I do not think that even the more excruciating bores and defenders of virtue (who always believe that virtue is their monopoly and are, at the bottom of their hearts, offended if anyone else dares to practise it) misunderstood him. He had nothing against the Encyclopaedia Britannica (in fact he worked for that publication) but he abhorred people who just sat down to read the Encyclopaedia. (He would have abhorred me, too.) Once he spoke of Haiti . . . (he spelt it Hayti). "Bull fights, cock fights, pig fights, are openly permitted. Business never begins till eleven in the morning. Everybody sleeps after lunch, and the bars remain open all night. Marriage is but a casual relation. In fact, the general condition of morality, so they tell me, is lower in Hayti than it has been anywhere since the time of Nero. Me for Hayti."

In innumerable fishing stories he makes the point that no fish is ever caught and even that there was no trout in his trout-pond and no one ever noticed it. He was a great and efficient fisherman but the humorist—who wanted no fish on rather conventional lines of humour—was stronger in him. He could, as he often showed, get away from the conventional line, but it was in his nature not to boast about his exploits, only about his inefficiency.

"Successful men" were all suspects to him. He preferred failure. Successful men get so little enjoyment out of life. Ruin was much better.

There are many action stories among his works but he was much better at describing situations or a character. His observation was better and his sense of fun stronger than his imagination. He excelled in literary parody, in which he founded a school. He has many imitators even today. He was fond of describing a tense situation and then exposing its utter silliness—and our own silliness for having been taken in by it.

When the curtain rises on the psychological drama, Sir John Trevor comes in and lays his silk hat—hollow side up —on the table. There are the first few minutes of a problem play and the tension is almost unbearable:

"All this is done very, very quietly, very impassively. No one in the theatre has even seen a man lay a silk hat on a table before, and so there is a breathless hush. Then he takes off his gloves, one by one, *not* two or three at a time, and lays them in his hat. The expectancy is almost painful.

If he had thrown a glove in the mica fire, it would have been a relief. But he doesn't."

In these parodies and sketches of familiar incidents he can always tell us more than in his serious essays. He knows that the photographer who wishes to shine as an artist in his own right does not simply disregard us, his subjects, completely and use us as a theme. More than that, he is out to deprive us of our face. The picture must be his—the photographer's—likeness, not the victim's. He knows, too, that the real-estate legends—so popular at one time—and the stories of great money-making, are the stories of our own lost opportunities. "Fifteen years ago one could have bought the Federal Steel Co. for twenty million dollars. And one let it go."

It is surprising to find that his description of Paris and the French lacks sympathy and understanding. It moves very much on the surface and is only saved by Leacock's robust joviality. He said that in Paris the only place where tipping was forbidden was the British Embassy. ("Not only the clerks and secretaries, but even the Ambassador himself is forbidden to take so much as the smallest gratuity.") At the bottom of his *Parisian Pastimes* lingers the conviction that Frenchmen are funny because they are different from Canadians. They do such incredibly amusing things as measuring in centimetres instead of inches. Today it is rather surprising to read that in 1913 Frenchmen were also ridiculed by British visitors because they were much too fond of dogs. The explanation of Leacock's attitude is simple. He went to France where he wanted to make fun of the French but as he did not know them well enough, he made fun of their Frenchness which may or may not be funny in itself but is certainly not funny just because Frenchmen are different from Canadians. Leacock, however —many years later—was quite prepared to mock this very same attitude: "Mr. Smith, by the way," (he wrote in his *Sunshine Sketches*) "encouraged the use of the

French language in the caff. He viewed it, of course, solely in its relation to the hotel business, and, I think, regarded it as a recent invention."

Classic literature meant little to Leacock. He regarded it as primitive literature. He thought that the classics belonged to the same category as primitive machinery, primitive music and primitive medicine. He ought to have proved, one feels, that literature has progressed quite as much from Sophocles to Bernard Shaw as technical inventions have progressed from the ox-cart to the jet plane and medicine from leeches to penicillin.

Humour—its essence, its nature—always excited and interested him. He wrote an essay on it for the Encyclopaedia Britannica. It was not very good and was replaced in later editions. He kept returning to the subject but could not enlighten himself on the mystery of his own trade. His theories were refuted by his own practice. He believed that in emergencies people could not fall back on their sense of humour—yet this is what he himself often did. He believed that one could joke about funny things but not about serious events. Not about death, for instance. But a few lines further down he himself tells a few funny stories about the execution of Sir Thomas More. Yet, he adds: "The cold reality of death cannot be exorcised with a joke." He feels, however, the contradiction and tries to get out of it by explaining that the grimmest event becomes less grim if it is sufficiently remote in time. Well, it probably hurts less—but no tragedy becomes funny even after two or three centuries.

His theory was dead; his humour was alive. A humorist looks at things and he either finds them funny or not. But the humour, the grotesqueness and the oddity are not in the things: they are, or should be, in the humorist's eye. He does not joke about a major disaster because "it is not done", but because he sees no particular joke in it. But if he does, he should be able to make us see the joke. Leacock himself could be funny about his own old age and even lighthearted about his death. But he maintained: "Even jail is no place for humour." But jail humour—and often a very healthy kind of humour, at that—exists ever since jails have existed. Surely, if the humorist is of any use to society, his function is not to be funnier than his neighbour about funny things. It is to see the lighter side of serious, dark and even tragic things; to see sunshine in jail—real or symbolic jail. Everyone sees the lighter side of sunshine; a humorist is—per definitionem—a person who sees the light side of darkness. There are some tragic things which may render him speechless; but there is no such *category* of things. A birth or a wedding may be tragic. But death is not a tragedy in itself. It is as natural an occurrence in our life as eating, drinking or making love. Death, in some ways is much less tragic than birth. For one thing, birth and not death is the real cause of our unhappiness—if unhappy we are.

Humour can flourish in a happy world only—this was Leacock's thesis. To him, humour was only a symptom of happiness; I believe it may be the cause of it. He refused to accept the theory that humour could create happiness and make dark things look and, in fact, be less dark.

To save this theory, he added that while individuals could not be lighthearted about tragedies, "as nations we could laugh off our history". He did not know that this habit of "laughing off our history" is an almost exclusively English phenomenon. He tried to prove his thesis but couldn't. He told stories about the changing means of communications, about prohibition, depression, etc.—but all these proved only that he could tell stories well, and nothing else. I do not believe that we can "laugh off" anything. A planned giggle will not help; the right attitude will, nationally as well as individually. In the course of these meditations, he tells a story about a soldier of World War I. I think this story is truer in its implications that most people like to believe. "A dilapidated soldier, his clothing in rags, a shoe missing, his hand bandaged and his arm in a sling, was heard to mutter to himself, as he shambled away: 'I love my country, I'd fight for my country, I'd die for my country. But if ever this damn war is over, I'll never love another country.' " He wrongly believed that humour and kindness were the same thing. Although his manners were sometimes gruff, his humour was certainly kind and endearing.

He loved Canada. He believed in the British Empire which meant for him—good Conservative with egalitarian principles as he was—the co-operation of hundreds of millions of people not on equal but on decent terms. He admired the United States and had a deep, emotional love for Britain and Englishmen. He liked their modesty best. "An Englishman when he has to talk about himself doesn't refer to himself as 'I', but calls himself 'one'. In my club the other day a newly arrived Englishman said, 'One finds Canada simply wonderful; of course, one had seen India and all that, but here one finds everthing different.' What could I answer except to say that one was terribly glad to know that one liked Canada, that if one would take a drink with one, one would push the bell."

*   *   *

Stephen Butler Leacock was born in Swanmoor, Hampshire, in 1869. That was exactly the middle year of Queen Victoria's reign. Dickens was writing his last novel and Mark Twain had just published his second book, *Innocents Abroad*. Leacock's family were Hampshire people on both sides. His mother, Agnes Butler, was a clergyman's daughter. She had eleven children, six of whom were born in England. Stephen was the third.

He was six and a half when his parents emigrated to Canada and—as he put it—he decided to go with them. Fifty years later he went back to Porchester, England—the village they had left behind—to find the house where they had lived. He was shocked to find how poor and humble

the old place was. While not expecting much, he had had
no idea that it was quite as poor as that. "I felt hurt and
humiliated coming out,"—he said, and added: "As I came
out I saw that there were some men there, evidently a
builder and his 'hands'. They told me they were going to
knock down the house. I told them to go right ahead.
They did; so Stephen Leacock's birthplace was pulled down,
to his great satisfaction.

In Canada the Leacock family lived in the village of
Sutton, near Lake Simcoe, Ontario. The farm was a
hundred acres and the village consisted of "two mills, two
churches and quite a main street with three taverns."
Stephen stayed there until his thirteenth year. He remembered this period of his life with moderate enthusiasm:
"Our farm, with its buildings was, I will say, the damnedest
place I ever saw."

Times were hard. Farming did not pay. In spite of Mrs.
Leacock's small private income from England, they fell into
debt and had to mortgage the farm. The interest was a
heavy burden. They lived a miserable life and the children
hardly ever left the farm itself. Even the nearest neighbour
was too far away. Every now and then they went to Sutton
village on Sundays to attend service. Stephen was sent to
school in Georgina, a small town about a mile away. Later,
his mother thought the daily two-mile walk too long and
she kept the children at home. First she taught them herself,
later a tutor was engaged. The children and the family lived
a very scheduled life, but this was soon to change.

Farming turned from bad to worse and at the beginning of the eighties his father followed his "remarkable
uncle", Edward Leacock, to the West. Mrs. Leacock was
left with the farm. She managed to send Stephen and his
two elder brothers to Upper Canada College where Stephen
eventually rose to be head boy. A few years later, in 1886,
Mrs. Leacock received a small inheritance from England.
She moved to Toronto but, soon enough, had to return to

the farm which proved unsaleable. Her husband returned from his unsuccessful venture and "a shadowed, tragic family life" started. Stephen Leacock was 74 when he wrote about these events. His parents, of course, had been dead for many years. But even then he refused to invade the privacy of his dead parents and tell us more about this tragedy. "I always feel that it is out of place in an autobiography to go into details." Why?—the reader is bound to ask. And particularly why after such a long time? Many people write autobiographies in order to reveal such details and frankness has made few autobiographies the worse. According to some of Stephen Leacock's family, the reason for this reticence was not filial piety. The fact was that there was no tragedy. Leacock is said to have painted a somewhat distorted picture of his early life. His childhood was happier and easier than he said or remembered.

Be that as it may, a year later, in 1887, his father left home again, never to return. Stephen's eldest brother, Dick, joined the Mounted Police and Juin—the second eldest—also followed their "remarkable uncle" to the West. Stephen, at the age of 17, became head of the family but he was away at College. It was he who finally broke with the old farm, the "damnedest place on earth". He simply moved his mother out, letting the farm "go to the devil".

Toronto became "his own city". It was about one tenth of its present size and he knew no other town for ten years to come. He loved Toronto and even thought it beautiful which seems fond emotion carried too far.

He was happy at Upper Canada College. Having graduated, he became a school-teacher at Uxbridge High School and stayed there till 1899. He hated his job but was able, at least, to support his mother from the age of nineteen. He gave up school teaching at the age of thirty and went to Chicago—on borrowed money—to study economics and political science. Soon after he received his degree, he joined the staff of McGill, where he stayed till the end of his working life. He became Head of Department in 1908.

In 1900 he married Beatrix Hamilton of Toronto. His son—who lives now in Orillia—was born in 1915. Mrs. Leacock died in England in 1925.

He was already Professor and Head of Department when he wrote a number of short humorous essays, collected them under the title of *Literary Lapses* and—disregarding his friends' advice—published them at his own expense. His friends were not worried about the expenses, only about his reputation as a serious scientist. Three thousand copies were sold of the little book and one of these fell into the hands of John Lane, the English publisher, on his way back to England from America. He immediately recognized Leacock's great abilities, cabled him from the boat, bought the publication rights of his books and—as it was then fashionable to say—the Mark Twain of the British Empire was born.

Between 1910 and his death in 1944, he published at least one volume a year—and often more. His lifelong pleasures were work, billiards, chess, fishing and his huge house in Orillia. The village Orillia served as a model for Mariposa, the little town of the *Sunshine Sketches*, one of his most endearing books, one of the few in which he put not only his wit but also his heart. He was an outstanding and popular lecturer, too. He always hated radio—he missed a live audience and could never overcome his strong fear of the microphone. After his retirement, he undertook his last and largest lecture tour which turned into a triumph. "I had the most marvellous success here (Victoria) with a talk yesterday on *Economic Separation in the Empire*. They laughed and cried, just about: never was there anything like it, they said." But he never went on a lecture tour again. "Wonderful success—all records broken, but it's too hard."

The most outstanding event in his rather eventless life was the decision to go to the South Pole, as a member of

Stefansson's expedition. "But when he found that he couldn't take along his own supply of whisky,"—writes Mrs. Nimmo—"the long, cold nights of the arctic seemed too much."

There have been a few greater humorists in literary history than Stephen Leacock. But there never was a more endearing personality. Some may have been wittier; others may have penetrated deeper into the mysteries of human character and the contradictions of society but none was more entertaining than he, at his best.

Stephen Leacock was 65 when he finished his University career and retired from work; he was 75 when his time was up and he retired from life, quietly and without fuss: "Give me my stick" he wrote—"I am going out to No Man's Land. I'll face it."

And he went. But he did not shrug his shoulders and there was no twinkle in his eye this time. Death is a serious thing, not to joke about.

BIBLIOGRAPHY

Literary Lapses, 1910
Nonsense Novels, 1911
Sunshine Sketches of a Little Town, 1912
Behind the Beyond, 1913
Arcadian Adventures with the Idle Rich, 1914
Moonbeams from the Larger Lunacy, 1915
Essays and Literary Studies, 1916
Further Foolishness, 1916
Frenzied Fiction, 1917
The Hohenzollerns in America, 1919
Winsome Winnie, 1920
My Discovery of England, 1922
Over the Footlights, 1923
College Days, 1923

The Garden of Folly, 1924
Winnowed Wisdom, 1926
Short Circuits, 1928
The Iron Man and the Tin Woman, 1929
Afternoons in Utopia, 1932
Mark Twain, 1932
Charles Dickens, His Life and Work, 1933
Humour: Its Theory and Technique, 1935
Funny Pieces, 1936
My Discovery of the West, 1937
Here are My Lectures and Stories, 1937
Model Memoirs, 1939
Too Much College, 1939
My Remarkable Uncle, 1942
Our Heritage of Liberty, 1942
How to Write, 1943
                    BOOKS PUBLISHED POSTHUMOUSLY
Happy Stories, Just to Laugh at, 1946
The Boy I Left Behind Me, 1947

E.

3

"LI'L ABNER"

IT is difficult to take the comic strips seriously and yet is is impossible not to do so. In America they have become a social force of great importance and they have made serious inroads into Europe's intellectual defences. In addition, the claim has been made repeatedly—and sometimes by eminent persons—that the comics represent a new literary form. Some warn us that the comic strips are a social and moral menace of the utmost gravity; others declare that his new form of expression is capable of creating—indeed, has already created—works of lasting merit. Mr. Gilbert Seldes asserted in *The Seven Lively Arts* (1924) that Mr. Charles Chaplin and Mr. George Herriman, the creator of a strip called *Krazy Kat*, were the only two great artists in the United States, adding that *Krazy Kat* was America's "most satisfactory work of art". He went on to link Krazy Kat's name with Dr. Johnson's, "to whom he owes much of his vocabulary". Mr. Chaplin declared that for him Mr. Al Capp, the author of another strip, *Li'l Abner*, opened "new vistas of broad buffoonery with inspirational (*sic*) satire." Mr. John Steinbeck stated: "I think Capp may very possibly be the best writer in the world today." The European reader—who probably cannot have helped seeing a comic strip or two here and there—remembers the clumsy and often primitive drawings with the hideous balloons bubbling out of the characters' mouths and is surprised, annoyed or pained by such claims. Is the European reader right? Or is he, in his snobbery, rejecting a new form of literary expression simply because of its un-aesthetic and, admittedly, repulsive appearance, without examining its merits and shortcomings? Perhaps the new medium should now be allowed to present itself and take its modest bow; but it cannot count on a warm reception. Some receive it with polite interest, others with tight-lipped silence and others again with open hostility and contempt.

In the United States 50 million comic magazines are sold every month, and it is estimated that the comics have 70 million readers.

"Surveys point to the likelihood," writes Miss Frank, "that 98 per cent. of all children between the ages of 8 and 12 read comics. These readers come from all types of homes and cultural backgrounds, rich and poor, city and country, well-educated and uneducated. Intelligence quotients seem to make no difference . . ."

To this number many millions should be added who follow the strips in newspapers. Although their number cannot be estimated, but, with a few exceptions, it is an accepted fact, among newsagents as well as editors, that "it's the strips that sell the paper". In spite of the overwhelming popularity of the strips among children, 60 per cent. of the readers are grown up people. During the war the American P.X stores sold 10 times as many comic magazines to soldiers as the four other most popular publications— *Reader's Digest*, *Saturday Evening Post*, *Life* and *Time*— put together. There must be millions of people who read little else in the United States and it would be wilful blind-ness to ignore their increasing popularity in Italy, Germany and—to a smaller extent—in this country.

The expressions "comic strips" or "funnies" are—or rather have gradually become—misnomers. These picture stories are not necessarily funny—indeed, suspense and adventure stories are now in the majority—and as soon as they appear in pamphlet form they cease to be "strips", too. Their spiritual ancestor seems to be Wilhelm Busch's hilarious but slightly sadistic picture book, *Max und Moritz*. In America itself the early beginnings go back to 1896, to Outcalt's *The Great Dog Show in M'Googan's Avenue*, published in the New York *World*. These drawings were coloured in yellow of a most revolting kind, and it was they that provoked the notorious phrase "yellow journalism". The phrase, even in its original meaning, referred not only to the vulgarity of the colour—not much improved in the strips through the following six decades—but also to the almost impressive vulgarity of the artist. Soon the *Yellow Kid* and the *Katzenjammer Kids* were born among a number of similar attempts. The Katzenjammer Kids were *Max und Moritz* after emigration to the United States. In time, like all emigrants, they lost much of their native character and adjusted themselves to their environment. Today, the third generation of readers are still enjoying the first generation of Katzenjammer Kids, who are as alive and youthful as ever.

By the first decade of this century, the comic strips had developed all their essential, modern characteristics. They were neither illustrated jokes nor ordinary comic pictures with captions, but true picture stories. Narration and orthodox captions were replaced by balloons—a technical term for dialogue bubbling out of the figures' mouths. The balloon usually has a "string" to it, pointing towards the mouth of one character or another, to indicate who is speaking. Narration was reduced to such sentences as: "The next day . . ." or: "In the meantime," or "Back at the farm." Historians of the comic strip disagree whether the original strips were intended for children or for grown-ups. Did the children read them over their parents' shoulders or *vice versa*? This riddle may never be solved. It is certain, however, that in the early days the strips were meant to be funny and their only aim was to entertain. The main subjects of hilarity were naughty and uncontrollable children and henpecked husbands. Consequently, these early strips instinctively painted a distorted and satirical but essentially true picture of a society in which children and women are often the rulers. A reaction and revolt against this unpalatable truth was bound to set in sooner or later. It was in the late 1920s that the new heroes began to appear. Tarzan was the first among them, followed by a long and dreary succession, until, in 1938, Superman arrived. His one great accomplishment is flying. He can take to the air with great and natural ease and without any mechanical aid and, in pressing emergencies, he can fly through walls, too. It is obvious that America got tired of being satirized; people needed to identify themselves with supernatural protagonists and the comic strip artists were ready and eager to supply new heroes. The first supernatural hero, however, was Popeye, the sailorman, who was often riddled with bullets but never killed. Research in comic strip genealogy yields surprising results and reveals odd family connexions. Popeye is the father of Superman and Superman is the father of Supermouse, Supercat, and the rest, with a fair sprinkling of Superwomen. As science progressed the comic strip heroes had to rise to greater and greater heights. Today a fair contingent of them works on various planets—not infrequently in neighbouring solar systems—bravely defying giant ants or atomic swindlers. They reach Mercury with greater ease than we reach a London suburb during the rush hour. All this has caused a revolution in humour, too. The little, helpless and lonely man—as incarnated by Mr. Charles Chaplin's tramp—is dead and gone; the new comic hero is the Popeye type, as a rule more vulgar and much less endearing than Popeye himself, the rough and ridiculous brute who always has his own way and who, however stupid he may be, in the end triumphs and prevails.

The birth of the Superman and Tarzan type of hero coincided with the birth of the suspense story. In the old days the gag was concluded in the last drawing; today the story rolls on at dramatic speed and the reader is left in anguish, wondering, what next? There is only one way to find out: buy next morning's paper. In the meantime the technique of drawing has also sunk even lower. It was always extremely difficult to draw well in the small squares, in which the balloons occupied a large part even of that limited space. The best the more able artists could do was to give evidence of the fact that they could draw much better in more fortunate circumstances. Soon, however, they had to simplify matters even further. Nowadays villains are invariably ugly and terrifying, heroes angel-like and as beautiful as the ability of the artist permits, so that one single glance informs the reader—or viewer?—what to expect from each character. As the popularity of the strips went on increasing and the demand became almost insatiable, artists and editors racked their brains: new material and new heroes were to be produced each week. Old *clichés* would no longer serve; new *clichés* were needed.

The briefest survey of today's strips and comic magazines—the latter began to swamp America in 1933— proves that the horror- and crime-loving public is better served than the fun-loving public. Mickey Mouse, Donald Duck, other "animated animals" and Popeye are still popular and have kept much of their charm. Naughty children and innocently quarrelling couples still try to, and do, amuse. But the majority of the strips are of a different character and may be divided into these groups: Western, crime, sea, adventure, horror, science fiction, sex and pirate strips. Certain statistics, quoted by Mr. Seldes, based on 100 comic books and 1,000 comic strips from newspapers, gave this result: major crimes depicted, 218; minor crimes, 313; physical assaults, 531; sadistic acts, 87; physical monstrosities, 165. One comic book examined by Mr. Albert Deutsch in 1948 "demonstrates to the child reader how to gouge eyes with the thumb, choke off the windpipe, kick an opponent in the stomach . . . flatten his arch with the heel, bite his ears, kick him in the liver area, punch him in the spine . . . all under the protective title of self-defense." On one occasion an actual recipe for poisoning was taken from a comic book, and on many occasions juvenile delinquents have declared that they derived the impulse to commit crimes from them. In spite of this condemnatory evidence, one must not jump to a verdict of guilty. Are comic strips not used as scapegoats by some young criminals and a society tormented by a guilt complex? It is far from certain that the strips actually create fear and brutality; it seems more likely that they only stimulate anxieties that lie beneath the surface in a great number of children and which would be brought out by other means too. Dr. Lauretta Bender, Professor of Clinical Psychiatry at New York University and a member of the Editorial Advisory Board of "Superman National Comics", states that comics constitute an experience of activity. Their heroes overcome time and space. This gives children a sense of release rather than a sense of fear. In the child's fantasy life, continues Dr. Bender, using such symbols as comics present, he may be able to adjust himself to the world's trials and difficulties. Children's fantasies are no escape from reality but a constructive approach to it.

It should be added that even the lower comic strip should not be regarded as a general argument against comic strips, just as the lowest type of penny dreadful is no argument against literature. Even old-fashioned and generally approved fairy tales—with their witches, wicked stepmothers and supernatural heroes—contained enough debatable material. Besides, comics are also being used with the best of intentions for good purposes. They—as far as their effect on numbers of people is concerned—did more to unite and steel America for war than President Roosevelt's speeches. Bible stories were published as comic strips and sold in a million copies. Classics—*Wuthering Heights*,

Cyrano de Bergerac, *The Three Musketeers*, among others
—are also popularized in comic strip form.

It may be difficult to condemn the comics on their
obvious failings: but it is perhaps justifiable to condemn
them on their merits. For one reader at least, *Wuthering
Heights* in comic-book form, although it was done as well
as it possibly can be done, was a grimmer sight than the
sheet called "Horrific!!!" or the heroic tales of the Space
Cadets on one of the neighbouring planets. Again, though
it may be questionable whether comic strips do or do not
create fear, anxiety and criminal tendencies, it seems to be
beyond doubt that they create mental laziness and stupidity.
Mental laziness thus engendered creates a new market for
new strips; the new strips create more stupidity and this
vicious circle does not retrace itself on the same plane but
may lead into the abyss. If the comics are a new literary
form, they may well be a kind of literature to end literature.
It is a kind of literature not to be read, only looked at. The
comics may flourish and conquer; but their ultimate victory
—supported by their powerful and somewhat related ally,
television—may mark the end of the reading habit. It may
also help to create a society with two classes; the thinking
and intelligent minority and the strip-ridden majority which
is incapable of independent thinking and accepts ready-
made views, if presented by badly drawn pictures. The
growing success of the strips—as has been pointed out by
others—may, in time, create an added menace to democracy.

Do a few really good strips on a certain literary and
moral level—such as *Barnaby*, *Pogo* or *Li'l Abner*—redeem
the whole art? *Li'l Abner*, the best of them, although wildly
overestimated by many, is drawn and written by an able
satirist. His sallies are often witty and he frequently scores
a bullseye on his main target, Big Business. No one would
deny Mr. Al Capp's abilities. But the form in which his
ability gains expression remains, even in his hands, ugly,
unaesthetic and repulsive—and it is the form which is now

under discussion. Some critics say that the comic strips may give birth even to great poetry and that they should be given a chance. This claim is more than doubtful; and the new form has had its chance. It is a novelty more than half a century old.

" . . . I run into people," (writes Mr. John Steinbeck) "who seem to feel that literature is all words and that those words should probably be stuffy. The literature of the Cro Magnon is painted on the walls of the caves of Altamira."

Mr. Steinbeck may be right. Literature began with comic strips; if we are not careful it may also end with them.

SEE ALSO

COULTON WAUGH: *The Comics,*
            The McMillan Company, New York, 1947
JOSETTE FRANK: *Comics, TV, Movies—and Children,*
                        Public Affairs Series No. 148
GILBERT SELDES: *The Great Audience,*
                        Viking Press, New York, 1950

4

MR. PUNCH

THERE is one school of criticism which makes a distinction between the "pleasure value" and "influence value" of literary works. Baudelaire's *Les Fleurs du Mal*—according to this school—has considerable pleasure value but little influence value; while a grim sermon may have great influence value but very little pleasure value indeed. To examine the ideas of this critical school would lead us far out of our way. We should first have to decide whether ethical soundness is, or is not, an essential and integral part of aesthetic beauty; having settled this point as far as possible, we should then proceed to make up our minds on the once hotly debated problem of "art for art's sake" versus "art with a purpose"—and we would soon find ourselves arguing with Plato and Aristotle. Writing about *Punch*, however, I find the distinction between pleasure value and influence value convenient—so I should like to use it at least as a starting point.

Punch is not an artistic product in the same sense as are the works of other authors discussed in this book. *Punch* is primarily a social phenomenon. It is also a commercial firm and that involves the need for concession to popular taste, or what is believed to be popular taste. An artist may starve in a garret if he rejects popularity or is rejected by the populace; a commercial firm cannot starve in a garret or even in its thickly carpeted premises and modern company directors have, on the whole, even less inclination for starvation than modern artists. Literature today is not a seller's market. Every artist—even those super-highbrows who find Mr. T. S. Eliot a trifle vulgar—have to find a market for their products and finding a market always means making concessions to the customers' taste and other requirements. In the last fifty years the number of customers has enormously increased. Consequently the number of people who live on literature has also grown while the number of writers—in the true sense of the word—has correspondingly decreased. In a way the invention of printing was a severe blow to literature; the practical abolition of illiteracy meant the creation of a vast layer of illiterates who can read and write. The establishment of the so-called popular press was a further blow and the cinema has contributed its own share in substituting semi-sophisticated pseudo-knowledge for true and honest ignorance. Lastly television and the comic strips threaten literature with extinction. I should not advocate the abolition of television, cinema, the popular press and printing, even if this suggestion were more practical than seems at first sight. Television, the cinema and the popular press are good things in themselves but, as a rule, they have as little to do with literature as the manufacturer of buttons and tea-pots—which are also good things in themselves. It should be added, in fairness, that the "masses" have often proved that they are more intelligent and more interested in genuine art than those who cater for them on a mass production basis.

The writer who has something important to say (important at least for himself) and says it in his own way, has become a rare phenomenon, even rarer than in the past. This is the natural price we have to pay for literature's own industrial revolution. In the past, if you had an idea which seemed irritating, revolting or downright revolutionary, you could try it out in the drawing room, or in letters written to your friends and ultimately in some kind of publication intended for a limited number of readers. Today the drawing room is appropriately called the sitting room and the conversation is monopolised by a television or radio-set; you are considered—and probably are—a bore if you write long letters of ideological import to your friends; and you cannot send up a try-out balloon of thoughts and ideas in a publication appearing in a hundred thousand, three milion or seven million copies—and every line of which is carefully scrutinized by amateur guardians of morality and a vast horde of letter-writers. Our voice has gained incredibly in force; but the power of whispering has been lost in the bargain.

The revolutionary of the past was, at least in his inception, a solitary figure; today he has huge, organised forces behind him. Five centuries ago he was stoned; today he just will not find a publisher or editor for his work. In the Middle Ages he became a martyr; today he dies at a ripe old age, a grumbler and a nuisance.

Punch, being an interesting border-line case, is worth studying. It has striven gallantly and not unsuccessfully to keep up a good level; at the same time it has been forced —or so it is believed—to make great concessions to popular taste—not to the "widest masses", to be sure. It made concessions not so much to the advertiser as to "the old lady in Dubuque"—to quote the first prospectus of the *New Yorker*.

What has happened to *Punch* since its foundation 113 years ago? First, naturally enough, it has become 113 years old; secondly, it has been transformed from a fighting, satirical weekly into a cracker of mild jokes of an anecdotal and drawing room—or should I say sitting room?—type; thirdly it has become extremely respectable. Let us examine these phenomena one by one.

1. *Punch's* old age is partly a great advantage and partly a draw-back. *Punch* has been clever enough to foster certain sacred rituals, such as the Dinners, and the carving of names in the Table. It is no coincidence, either, that *Punch* sticks to its old cover—referred to, with somewhat

solemn pomposity,—as Richard Doyle's second design. A weekly paper throws away a great chance of variety and liveliness by appearing under the same cover for 105 years but *Punch* throws away this chance very willingly. In addition to being monotonous, this particular cover is also hideous and unaesthetic. I find Mr. Punch's face repulsive and radiating wicked stupidity. The little imps and elves— or whatever they may be—are even worse. The general effect is repellent and I find the ugliness of the cover the only motive which impels me to open *Punch* as soon as I can. I am sure there is not one single *Punch* artist who could not design a far better cover. But *Punch* sticks to the old one. It's tradition; and *Punch* deals in tradition.

Punch has become a part of the "English heritage". "Without *Punch*, England would not be the same as she used to be,"—people say. England, of course, is not the same as she used to be even with *Punch*; nor is *Punch* the same as it used to be—but this seems to be beside the point. The fact remains that *Punch*, for simply having achieved the not unconsiderable feat of staying alive for well over a century, has become the Official Representative of British and Imperial Humour. If you do not enjoy *Punch*, you have no sense of humour—so you do enjoy it, whatever the sacrifice. What is worse, *Punch* is terribly English and to enjoy *Punch* is the indubitable proof of your Englishness. It is like cricket. Cricket is not a game, just as *Punch* is not a comic weekly. Cricket, when the sun shines, is sunbathing; when it is raining, it is an endurance test; cricket is a stimulant; cricket is a sedative; and first of all, your enjoyment of cricket is proof that you belong to the Clan. It is a great compliment to the English that cricket performs for them the same racial role as the Nuremburg laws used to perform for the Nazis; but this does not make cricket a thrilling game. *Punch* has assumed a similar part in the national life, on a minor scale. If you do not enjoy *Punch*, the fault must be yours. *Punch*, of course, is not quite such a grim affair as a Test Match; but you cannot take it much less seriously.

Why do the English stick to their traditions with such desperate determination? I believe the two outstanding virtues of the English are their fair-mindedness and their common-sense. The English are rightly proud of their fair-mindedness (although it is not always the proudest among them that are the most fair-minded) but they are universally ashamed of their common-sense. Having established all their important institutions on a haphazard, unscientific, undogmatic, trial-and-error basis (in other words: with a fair mind and in a common-sense manner) they were surprised to find that these institutions worked well and survived. Survival thus became a virtue in itself—and probably it is, indeed. This is the basis, I think, of the English love of tradition and the ancient and venerable—whether it be an ancient Parliament or an ancient comic weekly. In England only the first hundred years are the difficult period in the life of any institution.

The other effect of the 113 years which have passed since the foundation of *Punch* is that the paper has grown old. This is not a self-evident truth. Oldness has nothing to do with age. A person may be decrepit, senile or venerable at the age of 25; and he can be youthful and energetic at 85. Or take newspapers: the *Times* is much older in age than *Punch* but it enjoys a muscular, virile and inspiring youth. Had the *Times* been established only last month, it would already be known today as one of the greatest newspapers in the world; had *Punch* been established last month —well, then it would probably be a different paper altogether.

2. When *Punch* first appeared it was the *enfant terrible* of British Journalism. It fought against injustice of every kind. It was revolted by the harsh criminal laws, debtors' prisons, drunkenness, the horrible poverty—and said so in no feeble terms. *Punch* was not only admired but feared;

it was not only a mild entertainer but a social force. Today the revolutionary élan of Thomas Hood's poem, *The Song of the Shirt* has been replaced by a mildly satirical, urbane and essentially conservative outlook. *Punch* today follows public opinion—or the richest section of it—like a well-trained, obedient and absolutely house-clean little dog, but it never barks aloud. It is on the whole amusing and intelligent but no copy of *Punch* is passed from hand to hand with outraged and delighted comment. People may read it or turn over its pages and look at the drawings but they do not discuss it. *Punch* is imperialistic, clean-minded, a staunch defender of the rich and a brave supporter of all accepted and approved views.*

No one should blame *Punch* for not being revolutionary or, at least strongly critical of the existing social order. Nor is it *Punch's* fault that it is conservative. There is no reason on earth why a comic paper should not be conservative. The Labour Party and Labour policy are not only legitimate but excellent targets for satire. But *Punch* does not really criticise; *Punch* laments. *Punch* is not fighting for a better future; it is fighting for a better past. Its jokes are basically against nationalisation, the Health Service, high taxes, the lack of servants and the sad fact that nowadays charwomen, too, may secure a better education for their children. A large proportion of the articles are written from the standpoint of a *declassé* social layer which is not prepared to face a new situation and spends most of its time crying over spilt milk and trying to save its own feelings of superiority by deriding upstarts—who happen incidentally to be the majority of the nation. (And they forget that a few generations ago their own forebears were upstarts, too.) *Punch* has ceased to lash out at injustice; today it only grumbles.

A particularly feeble and silly piece by B. A. Young (August 12, 1953) is a good example of this attitude. It is a Utopian story of the nineteen nineties and you can

* This piece was written in August, 1953.

almost hear the author's sighs between the lines. "Total Welfare" (sigh) is about Mikardo Hart, a meter-reader of the North Thames Atom Board. Having done five years' National Service, he is now looking forward to compulsory retirement at the age of 34. He contracts Neustatter disease —an urgent need to build numerous cheap houses for the workers (sigh). The houses become smaller and smaller while the ever growing diet of school-children makes them (the children, not the houses) larger and larger. However, the discovery of lunamycin (prepared from a rare mineral only obtainable in the moon) is a great triumph of national-ised medicine (sigh). After a long illness Mikardo Hart is forced to seek employment elsewhere (the Atom Board has behaved in a stupid, cruel and bureaucratic manner) but he cannot find a new job—he is too old at 30—and has to live on public relief (sigh). This picture—we learn—is built on a report of the *Times*, showing that the ratio between earners and non-earners is giving reason for anxiety at the moment and would further deteriorate. ". . . as workers became longer lived and healthier (I hope I heard no sigh here) they were encouraged to retire earlier." Con-clusion: ". . . though the suggestion may have been made in certain ribald sections of the press, it does not appear to have made much impression on a population able to con-template unshaken the sacrifice of half its income (deep sigh) for the chance of a free pair of spectacles." (Last sigh) Moral —as I understand it: abolish the Health Service and income tax, build no more houses for the workers and all will be well again. It is as simple as that, particularly if you believe that being a humorist gives you the privilege of being silly and irresponsible. Little wonder that humorists are not taken seriously if their official representatives behave in this way.

The "old lady of Dubuque" has gained the upper hand and she makes her power felt.

Punch is divided into two sections: one serious and one

comic. The serious half—reports on Parliament, essays on books and short book reviews, theatre and film criticism—are by far the best part of the paper. People who read *Punch* as a serious weekly review, will not be disappointed. The comic part is carefully segregated. The idea behind *Punch's* dual personality seems to be that there are "funny" subjects and "serious" subjects in our neatly arranged world and each category should be treated accordingly. I do not suggest that *Punch* should start publishing facetious book-reviews or theatre criticism; that would be unreadable. But I do suggest that a humorist—and particularly a satirist—should not be afraid of touching the most serious, indeed, the grimmest subjects. Swift wrote quite an acceptable satirical piece on a famine in Ireland and Mr. T. S. Eliot was talking seriously when he declared in Edinburgh, after the first night of the *Continental Clerk* that comedy is a better vehicle than tragedy for a serious statement. The humorist's function is to observe and point out incongruities and oddities which other people do not notice. Humour is essentially iconoclastic. And even the more innocent kind of humour should help us to keep our sense of proportion by pulling what is dignified and elevated from its pedestal down to a human level. But *Punch* feels sincere reverence for the dignified and elevated and its avowed task seems to be to make funny things—that is, things which are accepted as funny by *Punch's* social class—look funnier. Even so it performs a function. "Tis a good thing to laugh at any rate; and if a straw can tickle a man, it is an instrument of happiness,"—said Dryden. In that sense *Punch*, too is an instrument of happiness.

It naturally follows from this division of the world into funny and serious subjects that certain themes are not touched upon at all. To take only one example: sex. Nobody wants to see Punch transformed into a pornographic paper. But sex is not pornography and pornography is not sex, only a poor and pathological substitute for it. No one would say that the *New Yorker* is a less "clean" paper than *Punch*. Yet it recognizes the fact that a least some company directors admire their pretty young secretaries less objectively and unselfishly than one would admire a pleasant landscape; and that certain young ladies give their attentions to elderly and rich gentlemen for reasons other than interest in their small talk. I believe that a paper which makes fun of elderly skirt-chasers and youthful gold-diggers is not less but more moral than one which keeps a prudish and old-maidish silence on the subject. The *Daily Mail* has recently acknowledged that in our age "sex has come to stay"; and even the *Daily Graphic* felt compelled to make an attempt on the sex barrier. But *Punch* is silent because the English middle-classes—upper and lower—want their papers "clean", to help them to keep their children ignorant and prepare them for future unhappiness. I should not expect more from *Punch* than a recognition that the human race does not multiply by splitting in two like an amoeba; but perhaps that is going too far.

It is the remarkable achievement of *Punch* that it managed to write an article on the Kinsey report completely avoiding the subject of sex. It was called "Next of Kinsey" (*Punch* is in favour of such silly puns). (August 19.) The word "sex" is printed in it only once, in a reference to the Indiana University Institute of Sex Research. Mr. Kinsey's first report is referred to as the work investigating the "amative propensities" of the American male. It is a facetious article containing such witticisms as the following (referring to the order of appearance of the volumes): "It should have been ladies first, but circumstances alter case histories." Then the article goes on to make fun of the excitement with which the book was awaited (the piece appeared before the publication of the second Kinsey report itself). Finally it makes fun of Kinsey's publishers who—although publishers of scientific works—were obviously keen on making money. This is indeed ridiculous. One is expected to roar with laughter when one is reminded that a commercial firm of publishers is trying to make money on a publication. The most daring part of the article is the last paragraph. It mentions that the first Kinsey report sold a quarter of a million copies and adds: "Curiosity, like so many other things, is only natural."

There would be another simple way of bringing the paper nearer to reality and life: reportage. But reportage in the proper—or *New Yorker*—sense of the word is almost completely missing, although one of the best pieces published recently in *Punch* was a piece of reportage: *Morning with the Ustinovs* by Beverly Baxter. There are no reports from foreign capitals, hardly any from the English capital; there is no description of events of any kind; no portraits of living personalities.

What is left then to write about? First of all, politics, and I shall soon return to politics. But there is quite a large number of other subjects too. Once you accept—with joy or with a sigh—the fact that all fundamental subjects are taboo, there are still plenty of light things to joke about. The writing in *Punch* is on a widely varying level. Some of it is decidedly and annoyingly fourth form humour. For example:

Mr. Lennox-Boyd, announcing that a new edition of the Highway code is in an advanced stage of preparation, had a few stern words for motor-cyclists. 'It ought to be a matter of honour in every home where there is a motor-cyclist owner,'—he is reported to have said, 'that a crash helmet is used on all occasions.' It's going to look pretty silly in the bath." (Charivaria, August 19.)

Sometimes it is vulgar and in very bad taste:

"It is reported from America that the U.S. Army has eight thousand miles of war surplus rope, and would welcome an offer to buy. Failing that, would Senator McCarthy accept an unsolicited gift?" (Charivaria, June 24.)

But most of it is much better and quite a lot very good

indeed. Some of the old *Punch* hands are pleasant and readable humorists. A. P. Herbert is urbane, witty and entertaining, always has comething to say and says it very well; H. F. Ellis, Evoe, Kinross, Boothroyd and a few others are enjoyable writers in a minor key. And the drawings in *Punch* do deserve their fame and are vastly superior to the printed text, although they, too, suffer from the limitations imposed on them by the policy-makers. But at least they say briefly what an article would say not half so well in a page and a half. And the drawings often touch on subjects which writers would not be allowed to deal with. Fougasse, Punch's former editor and a frequent contributor today, is a great comic artist, so are Ronald Searle, Emmett, David Langdon and Nicolas Bentley. On the whole the drawings are the great redeeming feature of *Punch* and although I cannot possibly mention all who should be mentioned, I wish to add that Mansbridge and Anton have recently produced a few good, indeed, memorable pieces. The bigger, political cartoons, however, are too often pointless *clichés*. I have already said that the serious features are also on a good level. I specially like Richard Mallett's penetrating film-reviews. The short book-reviews, too, are better than the average in the British press and try to convey more information about books than that they are "readable" or "fragmentary but well informed". The leading reviews by Anthony Powell or R. G. G. Price are concise but informative essays.

Unfortunately, however, good single items and even the best details cannot make up for the faults of the whole. It is the spirit, the ideas and the general outlook that are decisive. Individual contributors can do little if the editor fails them. It is the editor who makes or mars a paper. The editor is the conductor of an orchestra of writers. Even Toscanini can do nothing with a bunch of hopeless amateurs; on the other hand, even an orchestra composed of adequate performers will sound different under Sir

Thomas Beecham from what it does under Stanford Robinson and different again under Toscanini. There are many promising signs that *Punch's* new editor—Mr. Malcolm Muggeridge, who took the paper over in 1953—is going to make it, not mar it. But the road to renewed greatness—or even to renewed life—does not seem to be a smooth one.

Mr. Muggeridge is a double convert: he was converted to the right a long time ago, and to humour early last year. His conversion to the right is more conspicuous than his conversion to humour. He used to be assistant editor of the *Daily Telegraph* and he is a highly cultured and able man. He seems to be fully aware of *Punch's* shortcomings in many fields and, I believe, he is determined to remedy them. He set out on his new task with great courage and self-confidence. He caused a revolution in Punch—and a very un-English revolution at that. The English genius is often able radically to change things without an upheaval; Mr. Muggeridge has succeeded in causing an upheaval without changing much so far. He was faced by the old, traditional forces inside *Punch* who had been half asleep as their writings and ideology showed but who now woke up with a jerk. Mr. Muggeridge, it seems, resented the fact that he was regarded as an intruder; and the old forces resented the intrusion. The new editor is obviously trying to make *Punch* if not a fighting organ, at least a contemporary record, and that is a very good idea. He prints many more political articles than before and this enlivens the paper to a large extent. It took some time before he found his own voice. In the issue of February 25th, he wrote an article—one of his first—entitled "Eden in Eggitto". He was afraid that the Suez Canal would be handed over to the Egyptians. ". . . it looks now," (he wrote) "as though the key which Disraeli so astutely acquired, and which Rommel was unable to lay hands on, will shortly be turned over to General Neguib, in the ex-

pectation that it will be safe in his keeping." It is mostly the
technique of this article that strikes me as odd. For the first
few sentences he remembered that he was now writing for
Punch and made an effort to be gay and lighthearted. He
began: "Travellers through the southern provinces of the
Sudan will have a vivid memory of the local inhabitants
there—tall, largely naked individuals, quite illiterate, and
seemingly unaware of the existence of football pools, talking
pictures, multiple stores, comic strips and other appurten-
ances of twentieth-century civilisation." Then he goes on to
lament that the Sudanese might be granted the vote, and
explains that they are quite incapable of understanding
what the voting might be about. Then, in a flash of anger,
he forgets his new role as a humorist and falls into a tirade:
"It (the present attitude of the Foreign Secretary) provides
a theme to which some future Gibbon surveying this strange
time will doubtless do justice—how, in the name of self-
determination and representative institutions, territory after
territory was handed over to as corrupt and pettifogging
oligarchies as have ever plagued mankind, and how, despite
this constantly repeated experience, each new essay of the
kind was greeted with the same idiot satisfaction and platitudinous good wishes."

Was Mr. Muggeridge talking about India, Pakistan
and Ceylon? I think he was. Such a piece will amuse nobody; but it warms the hearts of the Blimps all over the
country and the Empire. It is not very original or clever to
call your opponents idiots but, by doing so, you may look
a superior being, a least in the eyes of your less intelligent
readers.

The future Gibbon made another appearance on
August 26th. This time it was foretold that he would look
back on India (Mr. Muggeridge was reviewing a biography
of Nehru) and "note that the last dying echo of Gladstonian
liberalism was to be heard in, of all places, an Indian legis-
lature—brown, gesticulating men in white *kadi*, speaking

over-idiomatic English in quick accents, and after their fashion keeping alive an oratorical tradition . . ." It is very funny indeed that some people are brown and gesticulate. Nehru, by the way, is found wanting; years ago he was already "an almost perfect example of the shape of Sahibs to come." It is quite true that he failed to alleviate Indian poverty. Is Mr. Muggeridge attacking him for having failed to establish a Welfare State and introduce high taxation and a National Health Service?

In spite of the fact, however, that Mr. Muggeridge is an old-fashioned imperialist, a fairly new-born ultra-conservative and anything but a humorist, he has already done a great deal of good to *Punch*. First of all, he woke it up; something is moving in Bouverie Street. The direction of the movement is not quite clear yet but any kind of movement should be welcome after so many years of peaceful slumber. Then he is obviously on the look-out for fresh talent and has introduced some new contributors to *Punch*. A few of them might well have been left un-introduced; but Christopher Sykes, Noël Coward, P. G. Wodehouse and Geoffrey Gorer (not to mention the whole list) are considerable gains. Muggeridge has published some newly discovered limericks by Edward Lear and charming extracts from the recently found Boswell papers. All this is a great improvement. It remains to be seen how much the editor can and will achieve; he has certainly diagnosed part of the ailment and is seeking the remedy. He has failed to diagnose —indeed, he is unable to diagnose—the whole trouble. Part of it is his own trouble, too. He has to give *Punch* something to fight for; a battle-cry instead of the groan of the grumbler; an ideal instead of dissatisfied murmuring; a spear that glitters instead of pins that prick. He has to face the promise or disillusionment of the future, instead of bravely facing the past. He should go on serving the middle classes if he wants to—after all the middle class is a great and invaluable part of our society, second to no other social layer but he should stop complaining about free spectacles, high taxes and the so-called loss of India. In a little book of mine I once complained, in the name of left-wing intellectuals, about a shortage of dragons. "Here we stand, modern St. Georges, in full panoply, armed to the teeth and ready—and there are no dragons to slay." The shortage of dragons equally affects right-wing intellectuals, too. Fortunately, however, there are still plenty of dragons about. St. George need not act like a puffing, panting, disgruntled, retired army officer; nor does he have to slay geese instead of dragons.

3. I have dealt with *Punch's* age and its inclination to become a cracker of mild jokes instead of trying to become a fighting satirical weekly once again. Now I should like to say a few words about its respectability. This longing for respectability is an interesting and typical phenomenon of a somewhat disreputable age. Why, indeed, respectability? Why does Mr. Punch not wish to become powerful and influential? Why did he give up the desire to *épater le bourgeois*? Why not shatter and shock people? Why the morning coat and top hat instead of the clown's cap and bells? The answer, I believe, is fairly simple. We have lost all our accepted values and those that remain are trembling and crumbling under our feet. The Empire—to *Punch's* regret—looks like being divided up; patriotism, although still a great and noble force, has to endure the slow fermentation of new ideas: the idea of N.A.T.O., European solidarity and World Federation; religion is giving place to a vague and general ethical concept—people want to be good but the churches are empty; the symbol of Britain is no longer the all-powerful battleship but the smartly dressed commercial agent trying to sell goods for hard currency; and even sex has come to stay. We have lost our security and many people have lost their faith—without being able to find a new one. The left—and right-wing intellectuals who turn toward Yoga, mysticism, Catholicism, Com-

munism, or towards the vanished splendours of a bygone age, are all essentially in the same boat. Lost faith and lost security have been replaced by the outward signs of faith and security. This is an unproductive attitude. Bygone greatness could and should be replaced by a new kind of greatness. We cannot remain the First Power; but we can become the Third Way. No mean task in a world of fear and confusion. And no mean task for a comic weekly, either.

In the course of this little essay, I have mentioned the *New Yorker* several times. It is fashionable to compare the *New Yorker* with *Punch*—the one being America's and the the other Britain's leading comic or light weekly. But beyond this apparent similarity there is no comparison betwen the two. The *New Yorker* is incomparably more interesting, witty and informative. The *New Yorker* is the voice of liberalism, *Punch* is the voice of a ghost from the 19th century. The *New Yorker* is a serious paper which talks of important issues in a lively and lighthearted tone; *Punch* is a respectable country gentleman, cracking ancient jokes. The *New Yorker* is far from perfect—thank God, nothing can be perfect in this world. There is a new aura of snobbery growing up round the *New Yorker*—and many people tend to overestimate its brilliance and importance. Then, the *New Yorker*—although it, too, has made some concessions to the old lady of Dubuque—is essentially a product of New York and consequently alien to us in many respects. "England lacks a *New Yorker*,"—people keep saying. But people are wrong. England lacks *Punch*.

5

JAMES THURBER

"**H**UMAN" is the adjective which first springs to mind if one want to characterise James Thurber; it is, indeed, one of the *clichés* most often used in the reviews dealing with his books. I wonder if he himself would agree with the use of this adjective in the sense in which most people use it. The word human, of course, does not mean more than "belonging to the human race" (Oxford Dictionary) and "having the qualities of a man" (Nuttalls). The fact that this word has become an adjective of the highest praise, proves the conceit of humanity rather than its greatness or perfection.

"Having the qualities of a man"—is, indeed, praise of doubtful value, if we think of the qualities most men have. But as soon as we use the word not in an outright derogatory sense but attributing a mixed meaning to it, James Thurber becomes a very human writer indeed. And as soon as we use the word in this semi-derogatory sense, it becomes an adjective of the highest praise. Thurber is a human writer because he loves and despises humanity and identifies himself with it; humanity is good and wicked, magnificent and ridiculous, courageous and cowardly, brilliantly intelligent and exasperatingly stupid; so are we all—and consequently we have all the reasons for loving humanity because most normal people love themselves with a warmth, tenderness and admiration, unequalled by any other feelings of which they are capable. The real humanist is not the preacher who glorifies our virtues and slashes out at our sins. The real humanist is the man who forgives our virtues and loves even our sins. The man who understands that virtue and sin are the flowers of the same seed; that they are identical twins. There is no real wickedness in Thurber's world. Certain people have different points of view to our own, that is all. Ed Keller, in *The Male Animal*, is a man who has a great deal of money and, of course, wants to have more money. He is a trustee of the College in a Mid-Western town (probably of Ohio State University) and fights the Red Menace. (He fought it as early as 1939.) The Reds—whether real or imaginary—threaten his wealth and consequently—according to him—they threaten human civilisation. We all form our views in the same fashion. All we want is a chance for self-expression. For Professor Tommy Turner (is the similarity between the names Turner and Thurber a pure coincidence?) self-expression means the possibility of reading good prose to his class and introducing ideas of all colours and shades; for Ed Keller, self-expression means having more power through money and more money through power. He is not wicked; he only looks at society from a different angle from Tommy Turner.

One of his truly wicked men—who annoy and anger him—is Rudwool Y. Pettifoss who was responsible for the sudden, unexpected and seemingly inexplicable changes in Connecticut telephone numbers. New Milford 905 Ring 4, a pleasant number, was one dark day changed to New Milford 1006 W-1. The change, however, was only seemingly inexplicable. Thurber explained it. This dastardly outrage was committed by Rudwool Y. Pettifoss, who, working up relentlessly and maliciously to an important post in the Number Changing Department of the Connecticut Telephone Company, has now decided to get back at the world for what he conceives it has done to him. "He spends the day going through phone books looking for simple easily remembered numbers, like 905 Ring 4, and when he finds one, he claps his hands and calls in his secretary, a Miss Rettig. 'Take a number change, Miss Rettig'—he says with an evil smile. 'New Milford 905 Ring 4 to be changed to Pussymei W—7 oh 8 oh 9 6 J-f'." Then Miss Rettig reminds him of the regulations. "Somewhat mollified, Pettifoss snarls for a while, but in the end agrees to stay within bounds. He writes down all the tough arrangements of authorized numbers he can think of and tries them out on Miss Rettig. When she stumbles several times trying to say New Milford One Oh Oh Six Double-U One, he claps his hands and Okays the change. It hasn't been such a bad day after all, and Rudwool Yurmurm Pettifoss goes home in what for him are high spirits, to kick the children's rabbits around a while before sitting down to dinner."

This is biting sarcasm; a treatment never allotted to Ed Keller, a more vicious and harmful character. But Thurber understands even Rudwool Yurmurm Pettifoss. He had to go through hell on account of his name.

Another truly wicked man is the Connecticut official who thought of the trick that vehicle licences and driving licences should be renewed on different dates and not on the same day.

On the other hand, his virtuous people are never forbiddingly virtuous. His great-grandfather, Jake Fisher, was a great fighter. "If Jake broke a man's ribs or fractured his jaw, he took the man home (usually in his buggy). Often he sat up all night at the bedside of a vanquished foe, applying arnica and changing bandages."

He watches all weaknesses with tolerance; at the same time, his enthusiasm for progress and improvement is limited. Man—he says—in spite of his sins, stands a fair chance of lasting another twelve million years. It might be interesting to speculate on what he is going to be like at the end of that time, or even in one twelve thousandth of that time. Dr. Tilney, the eminent brain specialist, has come to the conclusion that man is using only one fourth of his stock of fourteen billion brain cells: only 3,500,000,000 cells. Dr. Tilney's belief is that when man begins to use all his brain cells—"in a thousand years, say, or ten million"— he will become wise enough to put an end to war, depressions, recessions, and allied evils. Thurber disagrees with him. He fears that then man would, indeed, become "four times as ornery, four times as sly and crafty, four times as full of devilishly ingenious devices for the destruction of the species."

Once he said—speaking of his failing eyesight—that he did not see double, only one and a half. This is also true of Thurber's mind. He sees one and a half: he sees the weak edge of grandeur; the silly edge of magnificence; and the shadow of greatness in the erring, tottering, small men. And he sees the vanity of all things, a futility behind all our efforts, dreams and high-sounding oratory. Often he expresses this feeling in the tone of light jocularity: "The effect of Thurber's letters on his generation was about the same effect as anybody's letters on his generation; that is to say, nil." On other occasions he asserts the same, more seriously: "We are trapped in consciousness, trapped by mortality, trapped inside an inadequate animal body, trapped within the poor limitation of the human spirit." In an interview he summed it all up with even fewer words: "I have never been able to maintain a consistent attitude toward life or reality, or toward anything else."

All these quotations tend to show that Thurber is a moral nihilist—but nothing could be further from the truth. You cannot take the individual traits of a writer—or of any man—add them up and expect the sum total of the ingredients to represent the man or the writer. Or, expressed in other words (the words of Mr. Lionel Trilling): personality is integral and not made up of detachable parts. Human traits mix in a chemical and not in a physical way, that is, they undergo organic changes while being mixed. I remember, when I was about 18 or 19, I tried to revive

the old attempts at establishing the science of psycho-
physics: to express all psychological reactions in mathematical formluae. Needless to say, I failed in this but not
because the task was too difficult; I failed because the task
was too simple. I got my formulae galore—but there was
always a *c* (meaning a constant) in these formulae and this
constant remained a mystery. You could solve it—but only
by purely psychological means. And if so—why surround the
problem with the superfluous paraphernalia of physics? The
constant was the real problem and in spite of the most clear-
cut mathematical formulae it remained as mysterious and
remote as ever. The Thurber-constant consists of a great
deal of optimism and faith and, however much disappoint-
ment, despair, and feeling of final futility is mingled in his
philosophy—basically he is a cheerful optimist. Take his
little masterpiece *The Last Flower* as an example. Any
summary is bound to do injustice to this piece, which is a
parable in pictures depending in no small degree on
Thurber's inimitably bad and irresistibly charming and
funny drawings. The world is destroyed by war and men,
women and children sink lower than the lower animals.
Books, paintings and music have disappeared from the earth
and even the few generals who are left have forgotten what
the last war decided. Love has passed away from the earth,
too, boys and girls only stare at one another. But one day
a young girl chances to find the last flower in the world
and with a young man she starts nurturing the flower—
and soon there are many flowers once again, groves and
forests flourish, love returns to mankind and civilisation is
reborn. Song comes back, towns, cities and villages spring
up, troubadours and jugglers, painters and poets, tailors and
cobblers come back, and so do soldiers, lieutenants and
captains, generals and major-generals and, of course, the
liberators. "Before long, those who went to live in the
valleys wished they had gone to live in the hills and those
who had gone to live in the hills wished they had gone to

live in the valleys." Naturally war breaks out again. This time the destruction is so complete that nothing at all is left in the world, except one man, one woman and one flower. Shattering as this story may be, it is essentially optimistic. After all, as long as there are one man, one woman and one flower, civilisation may and will be reborn—as, indeed, the story itself has proved. It will be reborn, to be sure, to be destroyed again, but it will be reborn after each destruction. The story is a *da capo sin al fine* tale; thus, the inevitable end is always followed by the inevitable new beginning.

*   *   *

Thurber's world is a world of small change. He rarely mentions transcendental, global and eternal problems. If he (very rarely) cannot avoid such expressions as "liberty" and "freedom of speech", he blushes and follows his allusions up either with a joke or with an apology or both.

A large number of writers are constantly worried about the fate of human civilisation and many of them are honest enough in this—that is, they believe themselves. I believe none of them. Human beings are made in such a way that they are all the centres of their own private universes and ultimately they are only worried about themselves. They are not selfish; they are only human. Civilisation is quite a big enough subject to preoccupy quite a few people; but should they get violent toothache even while atom bombs are falling a few hundred miles away, their primary worry will be the toothache and the fate of civilisation will be relegated to second place. Curiously enough, it is more often than not the pessimists who are tormented by the dark prospects of humanity's future; those who feel that this future is hopeless and that humanity cannot redeem itself. It is the haters of mankind who wish to save humanity instead of—more logically—trying to help it to destroy itself. And conversely, he who dares to think of himself not with self-pity or self admiration but with genuine interest, thinks, at the same time, of the whole of humanity.

Thurber is occupied with the small events of our everyday lives. How the bed fell on his father (when it didn't); how the dam burst (when it didn't); how coloured maids behave; how a friend of his mother's moved to Boston and how his mother re-discovered her in somewhat unusual circumstances after some decades. It is Thurber's ultimate paradox that these small and insignificant events open up a wider vistas and larger horizons than does the permanent whining by others about our dark common future. After all, the events of our everyday life are small events, not big ones. We are only very rarely murdered; the murders we, ourselves, commit are also few and far between. The bed sometimes falls on our father but more often pandemonium is caused because we just think it has. Dams, too, burst; but more often the inhabitants of a village run several miles in panic because they think they have burst. The important events of our lives are that easily remembered telephone numbers are changed, that coloured dogs bite friends and strangers and that we find an owl in the attic. Of course, it is also true, that periodically we destroy each other in gigantic wars and sufficient attention should be paid to that tiresome habit, too. But to be preoccupied with that habit simply means the distortion of the whole picture.

Other—and probably greater writers—have uttered impressive and hysterical cries which have rung, or will ring, throughout the centuries, in the long and chilly corridors of world literature. One was tormented by a feeling of guilt; others wanted to kill their Papa; and others again just could not go to sleep. Thurber, however, is the embodiment of human greatness, at least in my eyes. He has had a larger dose of misfortune than seems fair. He lost an eye in childhood; the other went gradually blind. Blindness is a grave blow for anyone—but for a painter or cartoonist it is the worst disaster. He has had to rely more and more on his

H

admirable wife and now—a few weeks ago—she, too, lost her eyesight (we all hope, only temporarily). Yet, Thurber's spirit was never broken. He may shrug his shoulders about the fate of human civilisation in twelve million years hence but he can shrug his shoulders about his own misfortune, too. Incredible as it sounds, he sees the rosy side of blindness —once he declared that it was an advantage for a writer— and is able to talk lightly about it. He does not complain about his loss; he complains about a gain. His failing eyesight meant that his ear had become much too sensitive:

"Even the sound of a wrist watch prevents me from sleeping, because it sounds like two men trying to take a wheel off a locomotive. If I put stoppers in my ears, the racket is deadened somewhat. Then the ticking is fainter and farther away, a comparatively peaceful sound, like two men trying to take a rug away from a bulldog."

*   *   *

Thurber is interested in dreams and in the supernatural —and the two interests often overlap. He believes—with his none-too-serious belief—in astrology. He is Sagittarius with the moon in Aries, and his brief biography, on the cover of a Penguin book, states that he "get's along fine with persons born between the 20th and the 24th August."

The Secret Life of Walter Mitty is about a poor, timid hen-pecked husband who runs little errands for his domineering wife, dreaming the while of true greatness—greatness made grotesque by its own gigantic, superhuman dimensions. He is the indomitable captain of a ship, a master-surgeon, a crack-shot, an ace fighter pilot and while his wife is buying a handkerchief for his running nose, he is facing a firing squad. ". . . erect and motionless, proud and disdainful, Walter Mitty the undefeated, inscrutable to the last." (*The Lancet* has used the term "Walter Mitty Syndrome" meaning the habit of abnormal day-dreaming.)

Another, somewhat pointless story, much below the Walter Mitty level, called *A Friend to Alexander* shows that dream is reality, reality is dream; that facts are mad and the sober person—convinced at last by reality—is "stark, raving crazy".

There is systematic belief, let alone idea or thesis, behind this flirtation with the supernatural—but it is again the true reflection of an endearing personality. It is never the experience which is dressed up as mystic and supernatural; it is always the mystic and supernatural which is brought down to a human, everyday level.

It is not the every-day occurrence which is mystified; it is the mystic that is humanised. The weary scientist almost sits down, inadvertently, on a lemming. The lemming calls out: "Careful, brother." The scientist, after apologizing, remarks:

"It is a source of considerable astonishment to me that you are capable of speech."

The rest of this supernatural story is a condemnation of our race—a jocular, light, almost flippant sentence of death. The weary scientist tells the lemming that there is one thing he has never understood about the lemmings behaviour.

"I don't understand," said the scientist, "why you lemmings all rush down to the sea and drown yourselves."

"How curious," said the lemming. "The one thing I don't understand is why you humans don't."

Thurber is much interested in animals, too, first of all in dogs. His dogs—whether drawn or written about—are perhaps his best known creations. His treatment of animals is, basically, the Walt Disney treatment: they are all humanised and their folly, violence and greed, is really our folly, our violence and our greed. A bear, for instance, kills his wife in the Zoo, simply because he cannot bear her loving kindness. Thurber loves animals, all animals, but sees nothing but the human beings in them.

❋   ❋   ❋

Thurber is very fond of facts and figures, too. It is probably his long association with the *New Yorker* which made him a fact-addict. He put his indelible mark on the *New Yorker* but could not free himself altogether from Ross's mania and adoration of facts and figures. Sometimes he writes long factual pieces on crime and soap operas— using his facts with skill; on other occasions he amasses the factual results of his research in a dull and tiresome way— but often he relies on them for his best humorous effects. It is perhaps the fundamental pillar of his method to examine the most astonishing and incredible occurrences with a cool, objective, scientific mind. He would never say, for instance, that his aunt, Mary, had an "amazing passion" for snakes. Or that "some people would find it curious that she kept snakes as pets." He simply tells us: "I doubt whether either of her husbands shared her liking of snakes . . ." (Note: "liking of snakes . . ." How many writers would have resisted the use of an adjective here?)

He relates great disasters in a factual tone, without lowering or heightening his voice:

"They were amicably divorced, without legal entanglements, and Mary (his aunt) all on her own, wandered out to St. Louis, where she opened a rooming house. It burned down, and she escaped the flames by sliding down a rope from a third-story window. Everything she owned, including God knows how many little tin stars, was destroyed in the fire."

He often stumbles on facts and cannot rid himself of their fascination. He speaks of a Mr. Ziegfield who came from a line of magnificent coffee-drinkers. His mother drank fifty cups a day; another lady relative, who lived to be ninety, averaged ninety cups a day. Mr. Ziegfield was temperate and rarely drank more than twenty cups. Having stated the facts, Thurber calculates that the whole family must have consumed more than three million cups of coffee in their time. "At my leisurely pace—three cups a day—

I have estimated that I would have had to begin drinking coffee while Carthage still stood and Hannibal was alive to have a chance of approaching the record of the great Ziegfield lady, even if I live to be a hundred."

The silliest statements are seriously examined and analysed. If he does not understand something, he tries research in the first place. His coloured maid, Della, one day, very early in the morning, informed him that there were fletchers in the garden. Fletchers? "I got dressed and went downstairs and looked up the word in the indispensable Century. A fletcher, I found, is a man who makes arrows. I decided, but without a great deal of conviction, that there couldn't be any arrow-makers on my lawn in the morning and at this particular period in history."

All this is much more than a trick; more than a means of achieving comic effect. It is Thurber's own way of looking at things: not taking even the most tragic or disastrous events too seriously but treating, at the same time, even the most nonsensical event and most idiotic statement with respect and curiosity.

Thurber's only play *The Male Animal* (written in collaboration with Elliott Nugent) was described, to my great amazement, as an uproariously funny comedy. No doubt, those who have seen it on the stage, are equally amazed at my amazement. The play was produced as light comedy and that was, probably, the right way to produce it, but to the reader—as contrasted to the playgoer—it is the usual mixture of fun and seriousness. It is a disturbing comedy; an amusing tragedy. The basic theme is the problem of Fascism versus Freedom: a young University professor intends to read Vanzetti's last letter to his class and gets into trouble. It also begins as a clash betwen the Rights of Men and the Rights of Big Money. But it is soon dragged down to a drawing room level and it becomes much more the private problem of Tommy Turner—whose wife gets herself involved with a football player—than the problem of an Age or an Idea. Here again the great problems become small and personal problems; but once they have become truly personal they become great again because the fate of freedom and civilisation is, ultimately, a private matter for all. It is a rather rambling but carefully constructed play, amusing to the very end and full of Thurberian optimism. This optimism is not exactly uplifting, yet it is in a way consoling. It shows that there is a spark of decency even in hearts in which we should have never suspected it. It also shows that the stupidity, obstinacy and vanity of some big businessman of a very bad kind may, ultimately, work for good, because as long as idiotic football players are connected with noble causes, these noble causes may have their powerful support.

*   *   *

Thurber is one of the most serious humorists; at the same time he is the only one who can make me rock with laughter and bring tears—tears of laughter—into my eyes.

His faults are rather the lack of certain virtues than positive faults. His subjects are many, but his range is small; his vision is original but neither wide, nor penetrating; his observation is superb, his imagination is poor. He grew more and more serious as the years passed. The nonsensical and uproarious humour of *Is Sex Necessary?* (written in collaboration with E. B. White) and of *My Life and Hard Times* gave place to a more sedate, even sombre mood. The early Thurber was a gay reporter on life in general; the late Thurber is a critic of it.

It has been said of him that "he has a firm grasp on confusion". If it is the philosopher's aim to discover a higher and better inner order where other people see only apparently unconnected phenomena, it may well be the humorist's task to see a higher and inner disorder in things where others see only system and orderliness.

*   *   *

In addition to being a great humorous writer he is—or used to be—a supreme comic artist. He cannot draw but that really doesn't matter. Purely technical merits or faults cannot make or undo an artist. Churchill, the greatest orator of our times, cannot speak; Balzac, perhaps the greatest novelist of all time, could not write; why should Thurber know how to draw? A dog or a seal may look quite different from a Thurber dog or Thurber seal; but this—we feel—is the fault of the dog and the seal. They should look the way Thurber draws them, if they really want to look funny.

It was by sheer coincidence that he became an artist and many of his famous drawings—according to his own account—were born by accident. He never learnt how to draw. He was fond of doodling, however—and he drew dogs and his curious unorthodox dogs became a menace, and a permanent source of irritation to his colleagues. The idea that Thurber's drawings should appear in print sounded fantastic. It *was* fantastic. Most people could see that he could not draw; but only a few realised that he was one of the great comic artists of the age, all the same. He himself tells the story (in *The Beast in Me and Other Animals*) that an outraged artist—whose work had been rejected by the editor of the *New Yorker*—complained about the treatment he received. " 'Why is it,' demanded the cartoonist—'that you reject my work and publish drawings by a fifth-rate artist like Thurber?' Ross came quickly to my defense like the true friend and devoted employer he is: 'You mean third-rate . . .' "

His famous seal on the bed was orginally planned as a seal on a rock; in another picture (the "Horsie"-one) the man was supposed to be standing alone but Thurber drew him so badly that he had to mount him on the back of another customer in the bar; a hippopotamus he drew is filed in the *New Yorker* archives as "Woman with Strange Animal"—because even Thurber's most ardent admirers refused to take his hippopotamus for a hippopotamus. I

think everybody knows the drawing of the couple in bed
with a seal climbing up behind them, while the angry lady
shouts at her husband: "All right, have it your way—you
heard a seal bark." Another drawing on the same theme
—namely that the unbelieveable does not become any more
plausible just because it actually happens—is a scene in a
doctor's consulting room. A terrified lady is facing the
doctor and the doctor—who is making notes on a pad—is a
huge rabbit. Says the rabbit: "You said a moment ago that
everybody you look at seems to be a rabbit. Now just what
do you mean by that, Mrs. Sprague?" In another famous
drawing a wild-looking lady (all Thurber females are wild-
looking) is crouching on top of a book-case and a man—
next to whom stands another lady of somewhat more gentle
exterior—is explaining to a flabbergasted visitor: "That's
my first wife up there, and this is the *present* Mrs. Harris."
In another, two people are fencing. One cuts off the other's
head whereupon the victim declares in a sportsmanlike
manner: *"Touché!"*

There are three remarks I should like to make in connection with these drawings which must be seen to be
believed:

1. Even his most violent pictures—*Touché!*—or the one
in which a coy and naughty hippopotamus has consumed
Dr. Millmoss—completely lack cruelty. They are charming
and witty but not repulsive or frightening in the least.
Death has become a joke; a "point" to life. "No one,"—
writes Thurber quite rightly—"who looks at *'Touché!'*
believes that the man whose head is in the air is really dead.
His opponent will hand it back to him with profuse
apologies and the discommoded fencer will replace it on
his shoulders and say, 'No harm done, forget it.' "

2. The drawings are more reckless, unfettered and
spontaneous than his writing. He never took his drawings
quite seriously; he is fond of emphasising his artistic illiteracy: he is most apologetic about it. It is as if his apology

ran: "I am not really responsible for my drawings . . . I mean my funny drawings as a joke. The serious side of my personality is my funny writing." This division amounts almost to a split: the writing Thurber is the good Thurber, the drawing Thurber is the prodigal son. He is proud of the writer; but for the debts of the drawer he solemnly disclaims all responsibility. As a result, his drawings are much less inhibited than his writings and give, in a way, a clearer insight into Thurber's world. It is a grotesque and charming world, where the impossible happens, where naked ladies play the piano to embarrassed guests, where respectable family doctors fly in the air, where little repulsive female monsters pray that . . . "and keep me a normal, healthy girl" and where a drunken husband, carrying a rabbit, offers the clear, logical and uncontradictable explanation to his wife: "Darling, I seem to have this rabbit." It is Thurber's world without any make-up. In his later and more serious years he gave up drawing. It was because of his failing eyesight—the result of a misfortune. But in spite of his apparent struggle to persevere—for some time he drew on huge pieces of paper—he was probably quite pleased to give it up. The prodigal son was banished; the black sheep of the family was expelled not by him but by cruel circumstances. But there is no real coincidence in life.

3. The truth is that Thurber the writer was jealous of Thurber the artist. The latter almost stole the limelight. Thurber—the man without much vanity—was always deeply offended when people who only knew his drawings, asked him with surprise: "Oh, you also write?" He said (according to *Time*, July 9, 1951): "The human species is both horrible and wonderful. Occasionally I get very mad at human beings, but there's nothing you can do about it. I like people and hate them at the same time. I wouldn't draw them in cartoons, if I didn't think they were horrible; and I wouldn't write about them if I didn't think they were wonderful."

James Grover Thurber was born in December 1894 in Columbus, Ohio. He was the second of three sons.

We now know a great deal about his family. Many people refuse to believe his account of his forebears—I believe them without hesitation. His maternal great grandfather, Jake Fisher, was a man of almost incredible physical strength. He could lift a horse and—apparently—often did lift horses. In his blacksmith's shop, for some inscrutable reason, he found it easier to lift them than to lead them. In fights he lifted people and threw them. (He never threw horses it seems.) He could—and often did—throw a grown up man as far as 25 feet. He only fought with his fists in political and religious disputes. Mostly religious, I should think. In his seventies Jake Fisher could still lift 200 pounds dead weight from the ground and hold it at arm's length above his head. James did not inherit his great-grandfather's strength but he inherited his wisdom. When the old man lay on his deathbed, a preacher called and asked him whether he wished to forgive his enemies. He replied: "I ain't got none. I licked 'em all."

His grandfather always tried to cover up embarrassing situations by offering people watermelons. His—Thurber's —father, Charles Thurber, lost *his* father in a riding accident when he was a few months old. Charles Thurber had to earn his livelihood as a child. He sold newspapers in Indianapolis: "Everybody's father is a great, good man, someone has said, and mine was no exception." Charles Thurber became a successful businessman and a rather unsuccessful politician. He kept running for various offices but he was never elected to any. He became secretary to two governors of Ohio and to a mayor of Columbus. He was, probably, much too honest to make a really successful politician; he was altogether much too honest for almost anything. He loved, among other things, newspaper contests and at one period he invented certain contests of his own. "He sold some contests to newspapers in the Middle West but once a contest manager suggested that they should set up a phoney winner and divide the prize. He stalked out of the manager's office and his work on contests ended that day." Whenever he was worried or felt frustrated he would brush his hair for five minutes or would take a train to Indianapolis and walk along Lockerbie Street. Neither brushing the hair, nor the walk in Lockerbie Street can be called a violent reaction.

Mary Agnes Fisher, Thurber's mother, was 86 when Thurber wrote his Album. She refused to wear black because "Black is for old ladies." At that age she was engaged in writing a cookery book and her first play.

Thurber himself began to write at the age of ten and to draw at fourteen; according to other sources he began to draw at ten and to write only much later. I am afraid I am unable to clear up this point for posterity.

At the age of six he lost an eye but he has never described this accident. The reason for his silence is his good nature and tact: the accident was caused by one of his brothers who shot his eye out with an arrow.

Thurber attended Ohio State University but left in the senior year to become a code clerk first in Washington and later in Paris, during the years 1918-1920. Back in Ohio, he became a newspaper man on the Columbus *Dispatch* and afterwards got a post for himself on the Paris edition of the *Chicago Tribune*. The *New Yorker* was a very young paper when Thurber—back once again in the United States—started bombarding Ross, its editor, with manuscripts. Some were accepted and Ross eventually engaged him but, to Thurber's great surprise and horror, as managing editor. By the end of his first six months on the *New Yorker* he had succeeded in working his way down (or up?) to a small editorial post. In 1922 he married Althea Adams of Columbus. The Thurbers had a daughter, Rosemary. This marriage was dissolved after twelve years and in 1935 he married his present wife, Helen Wismer. The Thurbers now live in Connecticut. Thurber went through a number of serious eye operations but the surgeon could not save his second eye. He is almost totally blind but even now he sees more than most of us.

This very articulate writer—the bulk of whose writing is autobiographical—has never complained about his misfortune. There is not a single word in his writings tinged with self-pity or complaint. In 1951 he was made an honorary doctor of literature of Williams College, Williamstown.

Robert M. Coates describes Thurber: "Tall, shy, loose-jointed, and absent-minded, he has the physical equipment for getting into involuntary mischief and the artist's detachment for making the most of it after it has happened."

Elliott Nugent writes: "Unstimulated he is the mildest of men. When a cloud is over him, he reacts to nothing. Even with friends he is shy and reluctant to disagree when in this mood of low vitality . . .The whirlwind comes later. Suddenly the mild, patient Thurber is gone like a forgotten zephyr, and a new piercing hurricane is upon you, piling up waves of argument and invective . . . Next day, while you are patching your sails and cutting away the wreckage, Thurber appears in a canoe, bearing fruit and flowers."

*   *   *

I never met Thurber although he was the only one of my humorists I wanted to meet. The others I may admire or not; I may like them or not; but Thurber is the only one I love. Mr. William Shawn, the present editor of the *New Yorker*, was kind enough to try and arrange an appointment for me in the Spring of 1953 but Thurber was not well enough to meet strange admirers. I had learnt my lesson on Literary Pilgrimage. I had learnt it from him:

"Rule X. If on your arrival, the door is opened by a member of the literary figure's household who says that the Master will not be able to see you for forty-eight hours, do not hang around the house or the neighbourhood. Go away.

"Rule XI. If, in such a case, you do go away, do not leave behind for the distinguished writer to read, a thousand word note written in longhand and beginning, 'In 1908, when my brother-in-law was an oiler on a Danish cattle-boat, he found one of your . . . etc.' Don't leave any note at all. Just go away.

"Rule XII. And stay away."

So I went away.
And stayed away.

BIBLIOGRAPHY

Is Sex Necessary? (with E. B. White), 1929
The Owl in the Attic, 1931
The Seal in the Bedroom, 1932
My Life and Hard Times, 1933
The Middle-Aged Man on the Flying Trapeze, 1935
Let Your Mind Alone, 1937
The Cream of Thurber, 1939
The Male Animal (a play, with E. Nugent), 1940
Fables of Our Times, 1940
My World and Welcome to It, 1942
The Great Quillow, 1943
Men, Women and Dogs, 1944
The Thurber Carnival, 1945
The White Deer, 1945
The Beast in Me and Other Animals, 1948
The Thirteen Clocks, 1950
The Thurber Album, 1952
Thurber Country, 1953

6

EVELYN WAUGH

I T was twenty-six years ago, in 1928, that Mr. Evelyn Waugh's first novel was published.

Decline and Fall was the title of this first novel, and *Decline and Fall* would be an appropriate title or motto for Mr. Waugh's entire *oeuvre*. Not because Mr. Waugh is declining and falling as a writer, as some of his critics wrongly allege; but because decline and fall are his main theme. I believe that the human race is capable of almost infinite decline without an ultimate fall; indeed, that through its decline it can reach ever new heights. Mr. Waugh believes that the decline is bound to end in catastrophe and first the diagnosis, later the therapeutics of this disease have occupied his mind

He is a controversial writer and is likely to remain so for a long time. He is one of the most outstanding authors of these decades. He is a comic genius. Many critics in the daily and weekly papers are simply annoyed with him: he used to entertain them and now they think he has ceased to be funny. The early Waugh tickled them and roused them to happy laughter and the later Waugh fails to; so Mr. Waugh is admonished to give up his newly adopted role of preacher and purifier of morals and return to his early themes and moods. For them it is as simple as that: they see two Waughs where there is only one.

Others accept this judgment but add something to it. The break was caused—they maintain—by Evelyn Waugh's conversion to Catholicism. It is since his conversion that he has become a moralist. Catholic philosophy, the Catholic way, or rather view of life, angers and disturbs these critics and they cease to judge Waugh as a writer, They try to regard his novels as moralist tracts or Catholic propaganda which they of course—without losing their literary qualities —indeed are. But every book—whoever writes it—is a moralist tract and propaganda for one thing or another. Mr. Waugh's Catholicism—these critics go on—should be his own private affair, why drag it into his writing? But all the convictions and beliefs—indeed, all the utterences of all writers were and are the private affairs of authors; private affairs disclosed to millions. To accept a writer without his basic beliefs is like accepting pineapple without its taste or accepting a song without its melody. Catholic writers and the Catholic press, on the other hand, realize that Mr. Waugh is a popular novelist; a Catholic convert; a first-class propagandist; and consequently a great asset to them. They acclaim the Catholic and try to inflate the writer, whatever he may publish. The fact remains that Evelyn Waugh's Catholicism has always been an essential ingredient of his mental make-up; his Catholicism, in an embryonic state, was present, though not then apparent even in his earliest and most uproarious works, before his conversion.

If—as I believe—it is true that he is the bard of decline and fall, then there is no break in his career, no divergence from the original line; there is only a straight and logical —although not altogether happy—development.

＊   ＊   ＊

There are three more or less distinct phases in Mr. Evelyn Waugh's development. The first was the era of lighthearted slapstick, Puckish humour; then his humour became blended with a misanthropic streak and increased in bitterness; finally a new theme appeared, the Search—the vain Search—for Goodness. All such classifications are more or less artificial and dogmatic; not true in all respects but helpful for understanding. Clear boundaries are lacking between these phases and the periods overlap. His most serious works abound in uproarious scenes; while his earliest and funniest novels were, in fact, variations on basically serious and bitter themes. *Men at Arms*—the first volume of a trilogy—is not a Catholic novel but it is soaked in, and impregnated with, Catholicism; *Helena*, about Constantine's mother, the discoverer of the true Cross, his most serious, most pious, historical novel, is full of dialogues such as this: "Homoiousion is definitely dated. *Everyone* who really counts is for homoousion—or is it the other way round?" (The spirit of Mayfair, apparently, is as old and eternal as the spirit of Christianity.)

In the early novels, Mr. Waugh described his disillusioned, dissolute and aimlessly floating age not only with humour but with gusto and enthusiasm. He stated a case, or rather painted a picture but expressed no moral judgment. He did not condemn his worthless young men, or elderly rakes and sinners, nor were they worried in the least by a feeling of guilt. They were not presented as moral or immoral, they were, if anything, amoral. Amoral like flowers—flowers of a certain climate.

He was dissatisfied with this kind of presentation and his dislike of humanity became more and more apparent. But misanthropy is only a projection of self-hatred, so it is no solution. It is not even a problem, only the semblance of a problem. In this era he moved away from humorous writing and his novels became gradually more conventional (not in the derogatory sense of the word).

* * *

Not that our decline was a gloomy affair. On the contrary, it was simply delightful. Mr. Waugh's audacity and the gay disgust with which he observed the world around him were most captivating. His heroes and minor characters were all types but freshly an dindividually observed types. And are not all characters around us types? Do they not all represent motives driving them to act wisely or foolishly, in a cowardly or brave fashion—but mostly foolishly and in a cowardly way? Do not all people represent certain layers of society as well as ideas—meagre and uninspiring as these ideas may be? The tale of 2,200 million unique and divine individuals is humbug; there are 2,200 million types on this earth. We are all composed of the same ingredients and it is only slight variations in the doses of these ingredients and the way they mix chemically that produce such multifarious and odd results.

In the first novels (*Decline and Fall* and *Vile Bodies*) we were shown a bright and dissolute Mayfair, the world of night clubs, country aristocracy and lordly mansions— a world happily unaware of its own rottenness; in *Scoop* and *Black Mischief* we were taken among more real savages but the writer and his readers were never quite sure who the real savages were: the black natives of Azania or the civilising white intruders. "The theme of the decline of society," —writes Mr. Edmund Wilson—"is here (in *Black Mischief*) not presented merely in terms of night club London: it is symbolized by the submergence of the white man in the black savagery he is trying to exploit." It is not the black savages who, in the end, eat up Basil Seal for supper; it is Basil Seal who consumes unawares his own beloved girl at a savage feast. *A Handful of Dust*—Waugh's best book up to that time—returns to England but ends again in the wilderness of Brazil. Brenda Last and her Mr. Beaver behave with utter selfishness and lack of scruples; the illiterate, half-Indian Mr. Todd, who keeps Anthony Last, the English aristocrat, prisoner, treats him with the utmost courtesy, almost with love, and keeps him in captivity only to force him to read Dickens aloud. Todd would shoot Tony without much ado if he tried to escape but he sobs bitterly over *Bleak House* and *Little Dorrit*—however often he may have heard these stories. Tony—lying ill in the tropical jungles of Brazil—exclaims in his feverish dreams: "Let us kill in the gentlest manner. I will tell you what I have learnt in the forest, where time is different. There is no City. Mrs. Beaver has covered it with chromium plating and converted it into flats. Three guineas a week, each with a separate bathroom. Very suitable for base love." The wild prairies of Brazil signify a definite improvement on barbarous Mayfair.

The Loved One reached new heights. Waugh was now writing with greater assurance and increasing bitterness; he described only essentials and his characters conformed more consistently to the rules and laws of his own mad, sad and funny world.

Death has become a flourishing trade and the funeral services seek to be as smooth and efficient as the services of a first-class hotel. The task of the mortuary cosmetician is discussed with gusto and great expert knowledge. Aimée—a junior at Whispering Glades—talks about Mr. Joyboy, the main cosmetician with pride and admiration: "Why, if he'd sat on an atom bomb (the Loved One, to be buried) they'd make him presentable."

What should a corpse wear in its coffin? "You see we can fit a Loved One out very reasonably as a casket suit does not have to be designed for hard wear and in cases where only the upper part is exposed for leave-taking there is no need for more than a jacket and vest."

Dennis was quite justified in answering: "Sir Francis was not much of a dandy. I doubt of his having anything quite suitable for casket wear."

At last he gets good advice:

"We usually recommend the casket half-exposure for gentlemen because the legs never look so well."

The experts do not forget anything. "The monocle looks less natural when the eye is closed."

Mr. Joyboy was a master cosmetician. Not a mere theorist. "He had only to be seen with a corpse to be respected." He was in love with Aimée and he made all the corpses he sent up to her for shampooing, shaving and manicuring smile coquettishly. A gentle thought: an original way to start flirtation.

These shattering and macabre jokes sometimes grow cruel. When I read, for instance, that Mr. Joyboy made the serene and philosophical expression of Loved Ones his speciality—"that and the joyful smile of children,"—I found it too much for me. Later Mr. Joyboy speaks again of his love for children. He means, of course, the corpses of children. "I try not to discriminate, but I am only human. There is something in the innocent appeal of a child that brings out a little more than the best in me."

I found that nauseating. Perhaps the fault is mine; I may be too squeamish. And although, as a rule, I find myself impatient with people who protest that this or that theme is not proper for humour, I find that corpses of children are not pre-eminently suitable subjects for light-hearted jocularity. Mr. Waugh, on the whole, has a very rough way with children. In *A Handful of Dust* he kills off Brenda's young son. When the news of her son's death is broken to Brenda, she exclaims: "Thank God,"—meaning that she is pleased that her son John and not her lover John has been killed. But at least this death is essential for the story. In *Decline and Fall*, little Lord Tangent suffers a slight accident. Later the author informs us that his leg has had to be amputated. Tangent is not mentioned again, this remark is made only to increase our merriment over the schoolmaster who shot him by mistake when starting a race at the School Sports.

Returning to the *Loved One*, I felt that it was Mr. Schultz—the owner of a modest funeral establishment for animals—who speaks Waugh's mind. Dennis suggests that Mr. Schultz seems to be jealous of Whispering Glades.

"And who wouldn't be," replies Mr. Schultz, "seeing all that dough going on relations they've hated all their lives, while the pets who've loved them and stood by them, never asked no questions, never complained, rich or poor, sickness or health, get buried anyhow like they was just animals."

At the end of the story Waugh distributes punishment in his own witty, audacious and cruel way. Aimée commits suicide on the advice of the Guru Brahmin. (The Guru Brahmin was two gloomy men and a bright young secretary in a newspaper office.) Aimée's dead body is hidden by her fiancé, Joyboy, in a refrigerator for "half-finished work" and is ultimately incinerated in the crematorium for animals. She who admired "right things" and "real beauty" —that is, the awe-inspiring but poetic ways of Whispering Glades—ended up among the ashes of dogs, parrots and goats. "Your Aimée is wagging her tail in heaven tonight, thinking of you."

What is the meaning of it all? Is this simply a macabre if amusing satire on the funeral rites of Southern California? For me—and for many other readers—*The Loved One* is much more than that. I have read into it a satire on a declining, half-mad civilisation which has lost its values and has replaced them by empty and meaningless conventions. It is far from certain, however, that the same was in Evelyn Waugh's mind. No book is *one* book; it is as many books as there are readers, plus one. This additional one is the author himself who is not there to explain and, indeed, has no right to explain. The book has to speak for itself and any fair interpretation is permissible. I am not sure that Waugh did not want to convey something quite different from what we see in *The Loved One*. Did he not wish to emphasise the contrast between the treatment of the dead by a commercialised, soul-less civilisation and that of the Roman Catholic Church? If he did, he failed in this, at least as far as one reader is concerned. The question itself provokes a comparison between the frivolously horrifying

Loved One and his most profound, most serious and sincere novel *Brideshead Revisited*.

In *The Loved One* we see that death is a trade—and why not? What else should it be in a capitalist world and, anyway, there is nothing horrible in death. Death, in itself, is not terrifying or tragic (in the classical sense of the word). The peaceful death of an old man, at the end of a full and happy life, may be sad for his family—but it is natural and even satisfying. Death, of course, *can* be terrifying; but so can a wedding or the birth of a child. In any case, in the event of death, it is not the dead but the living who need consolation; not the Loved One but the Waiting Ones. Whispering Glades, I thought, might have deserved better treatment. In a silly, commercialised and snobbish world it does bring consolation to silly, commercialised and snobbish people.

And what about the Church, on Mr. Waugh's own showing? In *Brideshead Revisited* Lord Marchmain led a life of sin. He was converted to Catholicism by his pious wife but soon after his conversion he left his wife and, ceasing to care for his newly acquired religion, lived with his mistress in Venice, untormented by any feeling of guilt. Many years later, after his wife's death, he came back to Brideshead to die. His family insisted that the dying man should see a priest. They knew that the shock might kill him as, indeed, it probably did. The priest, by entering the sick-room and bringing him the chilly breath of death was, in fact, telling him that the hour had struck. This may be in perfect order according to the ancient laws of the Church; it may be right, moral and in accordance with the divine will. I don't know. I only know that however divine it may be, it is not very humane. The people of Whispering Glades would never do such a thing. Whispering Glades means vulgar consolation, the Church gloomy and horrifying solace.

The dying Lord Marchmain—who had once already

ordered the priest out of his sick-room—now lay there defenceless but, to the surprise of everybody, not excluding myself—he accepted the priest's second visit and made the sign of the Cross in token of his final true conversion and repentance. But why did he do this? The reasons are left unexplained; so are the reasons for Charles Ryder's conversion. Ryder mistrusted Catholicism; Catholicism was the deep gulf which divided him from his mistress Julia: they parted because Julia was a Catholic—not only in religion but in essence—and Ryder was not; he regarded the scenes around Marchmain's death-bed as revolting. Yet, returning to Brideshead years later as a soldier, he was captivated by the spirit of the old chapel and he, too, understood everything. He saw the flame; and he felt that he saw the Light, too. ". . . the flame which the old Knights saw from their tombs, which they saw put out; that flame burns again for other soldiers, far from home, farther, in heart, than Acre or Jerusalem. It could not have been lit but for the builders and the tragedians, and there I found it this morning, burning anew among the old stones."

There is no other explanation offered for Marchmain's and Ryder's conversion than that they were captivated by the spirit of mysticism and were obeying an inner voice. But for the reader who is not a faithful follower, who hears no inner voice and who is not captivated by mysticism, all this means nothing and is utterly unconvincing.

What is then Evelyn Waugh's reason for his belief? His private reasons are his own affair; but as he makes his Catholicism the basic motif of all his recent writings, we are entitled to ask this question and try to answer it as far as such an answer may be elucidated from his writings.

Catholicism, like Communism, may attract many different people for many different reasons. Catholicism and Communism may be divided from each other by a whole world; but they are identical in one essential aspect: they both claim the whole man, the whole soul. Protestantism and Liberalism mean compromise; Communism and Catholicism mean unconditional spiritual surrender. They are served by those who are capable of this surrender; and they serve those well who wish to surrender unconditionally. Both doctrines suit people who are prepared to bow to the Whole because they have accepted a Part. That is why it so often happens that renegade Communists turn to the Catholic Church. Disappointed in one absolute master they offer themselves to another.

There may be many reasons for a Protestant's conversion to Catholicism. Catholicism is not one religion—just as a book is not one book; it is as many religions as there are and have been adherents to it throughout the ages. What does it mean then to Evelyn Waugh?

Charles Ryder asks Sebastian Flyte at one point:

"But dear Sebastian, you can't seriously *believe* it all."

"Can't I?"

"I mean about Christmas and the star and the three kings and the ox and the ass."

"Oh, yes, I believe that. It's a lovely idea."

"But you can't *believe* things because they're a lovely idea."

"But I do. That's how I believe."

The author, of course, must not be arbitrarily indentified with any of his characters. But it is quite obvious that he, too, strongly feels this aesthetic appeal. In addition to this, Waugh strongly feels that Catholics are distinct and different from other people. The are a superior and select group who always feel the apparent handicap and real advantage of their being different. They feel persecuted—which they are not—but Waugh, it seems, wishes to be persecuted. He feels guilty for the sins of the world—although sin, in the everyday sense of the word plays more of a subordinate part in his Catholicism than in Graham Greene's—and being the victim of an unjust persecution relieves this feeling of guilt to a large extent. A martyr is a person who *chooses* suffering or death; a martyr may be admired but he should not be pitied. He gets what he wants. A martyr seeks absolution or, indeed, happiness in his own way. A martyr is a selfish Epicurean on a higher moral plane and he regards his tormentors as the real sufferers. Evelyn Waugh wants to be persecuted and wants to suffer because he cannot forgive himself for his own way of looking at the world. He longs for beauty and goodness and finds both either in the past or in a select group in the present. In *Edmund Campion* and *Helena* he stands on a pair of spiritual buskins and can be incredibly dull. But his real nature break through all barriers. I have already mentioned, the atmosphere of Mayfair may be breathed in Constantine's court and Mr. Waugh can be very light-hearted or even frivolous about religious matters. Rex Mottram's conversion to Catholicism in *Brideshead Revisited* is first-class satire. Dennis Barlow in *The Loved One* wants, at a certain stage, to become a minister who buries dogs and other pets. He tries to get some information on his chosen profession and pumps an ecclesiastic who is dedicated to serve the souls of animals. This pastor tells Dennis that, to become a clergyman for dogs, he must have a Call. Without a Call the whole thing is no good. And he conducts the funeral service in these words:

"Dog that is born of bitch hath but a short time to live and is full of misery. He cometh up, and is cut down like a flower."

These lines, had they been written by a person of more impious and unhallowed reputation, might have caused an uproar; but Evelyn Waugh could get away with it. Only a deeply religious man is allowed to be profane.

Evelyn Waugh hankers after goodness and sanctity but he is always conscious of rottenness and decline; he would like to suffer because of this but he is only amused. This unbridgeable gap between his actual personality and the one he desires drives him to Catholicism and makes him hate humanity instead of hating himself. Humanity deserves his hatred because it is gay, lighthearted and sinful; and Catholicism means an island of goodness and beauty. The world seems to be divided between good and bad; so does Mr. Waugh. But the world is, in fact, indivisible; goodness and badness, beauty and ugliness, the spirit of Mayfair and the spirit of Christianity have walked hand in hand throughout the centuries and it has often been impossible to see which was which. Not only that black and white have co-existed; they are complementary to each other, one sustaining the other. Without black there could be no white just as without shadow there would be no sun. The world is, indeed, indivisible and so is Mr. Waugh. Yet, the satirist in him is in constant clash with the missionary. He is a powerful satirist but only a mediocre missionary. In his capacity of missionary he endeavours to convince and finally to convert one single person—himself; as a satirist he does not intend either to amuse or to improve us by making us laugh at ourselves. He seeks to awaken shame in us.

*   *   *

Evelyn Arthur St. John Waugh was born in London, in October 1903. His father, Arthur Waugh, was a well-known literary critic and essayist, a book reviewer of the *Daily Telegraph* and also managing director of a London firm of publishers. Evelyn Waugh attended Lancing School where the strict discipline, he declared later, did not bother him at all. Even then he must have been aware of his inclination to revolt and felt that this inclination must be thwarted by strict discipline, imposed from without. He became Senior History Scholar at Hertford College, Oxford University. Originally he wanted to become a painter and attended an art school for a short period. This was by no means a waste of time; even today he often looks at things with the painter's eye. He wrote a biography of Rosetti— his first published book. For a year he became a teacher and his experiences were related in *Decline and Fall*, his first novel, which brought him immediate and well deserved success. Afterwards he worked on the *Daily Express* and this period of his life is chronicled in *Scoop*. The 25th year of his life was of great importance. It was in 1928 that his book on Rosetti was published, followed by *Decline and Fall* and in this year he married. His marriage was dissolved two years later. In the same year, in 1930, he was received into the Catholic Church. In 1937 he married Miss Laura Herbert, the daughter of a colonel, and they have six children, three boys and three girls.

At the outbreak of the war, Waugh was commissioned in the Royal Marines and later volunteered for the Commandos. He served in the Middle East and was eventually transferred to the Blues. In 1944 he was sent to Yugoslavia as a member of the British Military Mission. There he seems to have conceived a life-long antipathy, if not hatred, for Marshal Tito. *Men at Arms*, the first volume of a planned trilogy, deals with his experiences in the army. In his photographs, Evelyn Waugh looks like a shy, rather aggressive and very self-conscious schoolboy. I have never seen him in life.

He lives in Piers Court, in Gloucestershire, "a shabby stone house in the country, where nothing is under a hundred years old except the plumbing and that does not work." He leads a more and more secluded life . . . On the average—he told us in an article in *Life*—he made one new friend a year and lost two. Even his children do not see much of him. "I have numerous children,"—he said in the same article,—"whom I see once a day for ten, I hope, awe-inspiring minutes." (Why awe-inspiring? And why should he hope that they are awe-inspiring?)

*   *   *

Evelyn Waugh is often accused of being a snob. He is, however, accused of this for the wrong reason. Why should he be reproached for writing about that layer of society he knows best? One could wish that more writers followed his example. It is not compulsory to write of the happy and deserving poor; one may write of the suffering and undeserving rich. Once he complained that to mention a nobleman nowadays causes as loud an uproar in England as mentioning a prostitute did 60 years ago. He was right in his protest. But he is a snob, all the same. He, the great critic and satirist, accepts the idea that being an aristocrat or belonging to an old family (as though all families were not equally old) implies certain values. There is no social criticism in his novels; the snobs are ridiculed by him but only because they are upstarts and try to reach the imposing heights of born arisocrats. He revels in the rarified air of lordly castles, he believes that the earl was born an earl and his valet a valet; and he believes that Lord Marchmain—an ignorant idler—was really an incomparably more valuable specimen of humanity than Admiral Muspratt.

He is much better at creating atmosphere than at describing character. Only a few of his characters are memorable as individuals, for example Charles Ryder's vague, ironic and selfish father who laughed at everybody with a wise man's laughter. His dialogue is excellent but also more true to type than to the individual. He can conjure up a personality before our eyes with very few words: "Ambrose Abercrombie was still on what his wife called 'the right side of sixty'; but having for many years painfully feigned youth, he now aspired to the honours of age." There is no need to tell us more about Abercrombie. And how real for us does the atmosphere of the American scene become when we are told that the secret of social ease in America is that no one expects you to listen. They talk entirely for their own pleasure. Many people think that a certain species of American girl was not born but mass-produced on the assembly line. Waugh remarks: "A man could leave such a girl in a delicatessen shop in New York, fly three thousand miles to find her again, in the cigar stall at San Francisco, just as he would find his favourite comic strip in the local paper." One could quote such descriptions and better by the score. It is his power of observation that makes him such a delightful writer. His vision—when he allows himself to see things as they are and not as they should be—is fresh; his descriptions witty and sharp. He often mingles straightforward reporting with wild exaggeration but you can always tell whether he is serious or not.

Some critics accuse him of using too many *clichés*. I think this charge is absurd. *Clichés*, up to a certain point, are just the small change of language and if some writers believe that their pedantic, breathless and always unsuccessful effort to avoid them makes their style more elegant, they are badly mistaken. A writer with a sense of style feels when a *cliché* is a useful and concise formula in the right place and when it is a dead horse, which will not repay flogging. Even the oldest and most worn-out *cliché* may gain a new meaning and a novel content if used in the proper way. Waugh can often say more in fifteen words than many others on fifteen pages—and who cares if he uses a few *clichés* while doing so? But it seems that Mr. Waugh does not think so highly of his own style. *The Loved One* is dedicated, among others, "to Mrs. Reginald Allen who corrected my American; to Mr. Cyril Conolly who corrected my English". Well, English is not my mother tongue and I cannot pose as an authority on it. But with my limited knowledge I fail to see how Mr. Waugh's uncorrected English—in his other books—could be improved upon. To me he is one of the living masters of English prose.

Decline and Fall was a young man's book. It was uneven; its construction erratic. But Waugh learnt the trade very quickly. *A Handful of Dust* was already a strong and pleasing edifice and *The Loved One* is a little masterpiece of construction. Not a word is wasted in it and the story

K

sometimes flows, sometimes storms to its climax. Waugh's point of observation is not a pedestal but an elevated stool. He is slightly above the heads of the crowd; he cannot see individual faces too clearly but sees the various groups and recognises their role and their significance; and he watches them with bewilderment, amusement and disgust. He has found his style; he has found his own art of construction. But he cannot find himself.

BIBLIOGRAPHY

Rosetti, 1928
Decline and Fall, 1928
Vile Bodies, 1930
Labels, 1930
Remote People, 1932
Black Mischief, 1932
Ninety-two Days, 1934
A Handful of Dust, 1934
Edmund Campion, 1935
Waugh in Abyssinia, 1936
Scoop, 1938
Put Out More Flags, 1942
Work Suspended, 1943
Brideshead Revisited, 1945
Scott King's Modern Europe, 1946
When the Going Was Good, 1946
The Loved One, 1948
Helena, 1950
Men at Arms, 1952
Love Among the Ruins, 1953

7

P. G. WODEHOUSE

MR. P. G. WODEHOUSE is the court jester to the upper classes. He is often irreverent—this is the privilege of court jesters—but there is no doubt about his basic loyalties and, at the bottom of his heart, he is always full of admiration for his titled fools. An idiotic earl is a superior person to a clever valet. He pictures the upper middle class and the aristocracy as they wish to see themselves; stupid but honest; foolish, extravagant, ascetically abstaining from work, and drinking too much, but hospitable, generous, truthful and clean-living. They would be shattered to learn how much better they are in reality. The "lower orders" are also delighted by this picture: while reading a Wodehouse-book, they can spend their time with Bertie Wooster or even in Blandings Castle, feeling always mentally superior to the rich and highly born. Mr. Wodehouse's other great asset is his childishness. He writes for the fifth form, or rather for grown-up people with mental age of fifteen. These people constitute a vast public. Mr. Wodehouse graduated to the upper-middle class and the aristocracy from the literature of school days and is a great believer in "fair play"—in the public-school sense of the word.

All this, coupled with his great literary skill and a wonderful sense of farcical humour, is the elementary explanation of his success and (now declining) popularity.

*   *   *

Mr. Wodehouse has written about sixty books in the last fifty years. Many of them have huge sales on both sides of the Atlantic as well as in many countries in Europe and other Continents. Several million people have read his works and his influence must have been enormous. Considering this, it is amazing how little has been written about him. Apart from Hillaire Belloc's essay and reviews of individual books, I have found only few interesting long essays on him, published in England. One is a brilliant one by George Orwell, called *In Defence of P. G. Wodehouse** but this is only half literary, as it is primarily concerned with Mr. Wodehouse's internment in Germany; another is a fairly informative but semi-adulatory piece by John Hayward†. In American publications, all I could find was a short piece published in that popular lower middle-brow journal, *The Saturday Review of Literature*‡ I read, *inter alia*: "Some day there will be composed a 'beauties of Wodehouse', like the now forgotten work entitled 'The Beauties of Shakespeare'." And later: . . . "my admiration (for Wodehouse) can hardly be described as this side of idolatry." This was written by Arthur D. Nock, described in a footnote as a "distinguished historian of the Early Christian period". The same number contained a review of *Young Men in Spats* and in this Robert Strunsky (presumably another distinguished historian of the Early Christian period) writes: ". . . there is one story in the present lot which places the author next to Homer, Dante and Shakespeare. It is called *Uncle Fred Flits By*."

Mr. Wodehouse is a good and conscientious craftsman. He writes with great care; his prose—including his seemingly loose dialogue—is anxiously polished and repolished; his plots planned with architectural skill and there are no loose ends. His range extends from light comedy to farce—

---

* *Critical Essays* by George Orwell, Secker and Warburg 1946.
† In *The Saturday Book* 1941-42.   Edited by Leonard Russel.
   Hutchinson.
‡ July 25, 1936.

and he is best at farce. His imagination is poor as far as character creation is concerned (more about this later) but it is an almost bottomless mine of farcical situations. When he is on top of his form, he is extremely funny and amusing; when below it, his permanent facetiousness becomes tiring and monotonous.

The external technique of his humour is based on what has been many times described as "felicity of phrase". People are "old tops", "old horses", "beans" and "crumpets". If someone feels miserable, then "misery has him firmly in his grip". An intelligent fellow is a "soundish sort of egg". Tea is "the healing brew". If someone is embarrassed and behaves oddly, then a "lunacy commissioner . . . would have made up his mind without further investigation." One person is "a human correspondence course in Efficiency" and another is so energetic and full of beans that "she would galvanize a jellyfish". Even funny derogatives are resorted to: "reptile . . . " "worm . . . " "blister . . . ". One of his permanent tricks is to point out the obvious with mock serenity. When Cedrick Mullinar tries to escape from a compromising situation through the window, the window-sash descends on the back of his neck like a guillotine and he finds himself firmly pinned to the sill. What can he do? He busies himself with his thoughts. "These,"—Mr. Wodehouse explains—"as may readily be imagined, were not of the most agreeable. In circumstances such as those in which he had been placed, it is but rarely that the sunny and genial side of a man's mind comes uppermost."

A more subtle use of the same device is Mr. Mulliner's defence of the smoking habit.

"They come to me and tell me that if they place two drops of nicotine on the tongue of a dog, the animal instantly dies: and when I ask them if they have ever tried the childishly simple device of not placing nicotine on the dog's tongue, they have nothing to reply."

(This paragraph also provides a good example illustrating how Wodehouse can hammer a point. It reads: " . . . they have nothing to reply. They are nonplussed. They go away mumbling something about never having thought of that." Having repeated the same point three times, it must dawn even on the dullest person that all this is meant to be (and, indeed, is) funny. Not that Mr. Wodehouse is aiming at the lowest level of intelligence, but he certainly wants to include, and has succeeded in including, the person on that level, too, in the large number of his admirers.

A slight variation on the same device is talking, as if the narrator, too, had missed the point. Mr. Mulliner speaks and a person remarks in the course of his story:

" "I said that smoking was dangerous to the health. And it is."

"It isn't."

"It is . . . I can prove it from my own personal experience. I was once," said the Lemon Squash,—"a smoker myself, and the vile habit reduced me to a physical wreck. My cheeks sagged, my eyes became bleary, my whole face gaunt, yellow and hideously lined. It was giving up smoking that brought about the change."

"What change?"—asked the Tankard.

The Lemon Squash, who seemed to have taken offence at something, rose and, walking stiffly to the door, disappeared in the night."

On the other hand, it happens on countless occasions that the most surprising, indeed staggering, statement is taken by one or another of Mr. Wodehouse's heroes as a natural, almost idiomatic phrase.

"Have you seen Mr. Fink-Nottle, Jeeves?"

"No, sir."

"I'm going to murder him."

"Very good, sir."

Wodehouse is wonderfully convincing with his understatements. You can open any book of his almost anywhere to find magnificent examples of it. It is not only the obvious understatement—calling the huge tiny and the unbearable not too delightful—which he uses, but also a subtle understatement in tone. He keeps a cool, matter of fact voice while describing the most hair-raising and ludicrous events. He is often philosophical in such cases:

"If there is one thing in this world that should be done quickly or not at all, it is the removal of one's personal snake from the bed of a comparative stranger."

He often works out a situation of great dramatic tension and then drops it effectively by uttering some idiotic observation of it:

"In all crises of human affairs there are two broad courses open to a man. He can stay where he is or he can go elsewhere."

Overstatement plays an equally important part. There is one, solitary snake in the bedroom, but the hero finds it "infested with snakes". There is one, solitary girl in Bertie's cottage at night, but he complains of: "every nook and cranny bulging with blighted girls". When Blashford Braddock wants to impress and terrify Osbert Mulliner, he tells him, among other things, that in Central Africa he strangled a jaguar with his bare hands. This is picturesque, but not picturesque enough. So Braddock adds: "I had a rather tricky five minutes of it at first, because my right arm was in a sling and I could only use my left."

Then again, in dramatic situations someone will suddenly start talking of irrelevant subjects. Even the inimitable Jeeves has a tendency for this failing. Once, when Bertram Wooster gets into a jam of exceptional proportions, we read this dialogue. (Wooster speaks first.)

"What a damn silly idea. The girl must be cuckoo."

"Feminine psychology is admittedly odd, sir. The poet Pope . . . "

"Never mind about the poet Pope, Jeeves."

"No, sir."

"There are times when one wants to hear all about the poet Pope and times when one doesn't."

There is another device, too, to which Mr. Wodehouse is inclined, about which, however, he cannot quite make up his mind. It is funny to speak of dignified and revered subjects in an irreverent, slangish tone. But Mr. Wodehouse would not dream of making fun of really important subjects—such as religion, for example—partly because he would not wish to hurt anyone's feelings but mostly because this would run against the grain with him. So he makes a compromise. Greek mythology is also a religious subject but few people are sensitive about it. So we keep meeting such phrases as this: "It was the sort of look Ariadne might have given Theseus immediately after his turn-up with the Minotaur." Racing—though a semi-sacred subject —is used in the same way: "He actually spoke to me civilly —a thing I'd have taken eleven to four that he didn't know how to do." (It is a recurring joke to fix the year by referring to some great racing event in history: "Ever since the scullery window was found open the year Shining Light was disqualified in the Cesarewitch for boring . . . ")

One could go on with this analysis of Mr. Wodehouse's external technique but to understand him better we must try to explore other fields.

Wodehouse is not a satirist. His mild satire does not hurt; it flatters and caresses. He does not even look at things with a distorting eye to discover the grotesque and phoney. He does not describe the world as he sees it; he creates a world of his own and populates it with people of his own imagination. Not a world as it is to his mind; but a world which would be funny if it existed. Perhaps some of the originals did exist in the Edwardian era. But no one else lives in the Edwardian era any more, with the exception of Mr. P. G. Wodehouse.

Emigré writers often have one peculiar trait of their

own. They are tormented by an unrealistic nostalgia for a non-existent world. A number of authors and journalists left—let us say, Hungary—in 1919; others left in the thirties; again others after World War II. Many of them are full of nostalgic longing—not for Hungary, to which they would hate to return today—but for what they still believe to be Hungary. They long to see again the pre-1919, or pre-1939, or pre-1945 Hungary. They refuse to accept the fact that the world has changed there—and more than once. Hungary, as they knew it, is dead. But the dead never change. The dead do not even grow old. Indeed, the only secret of eternal youth is to die young.

Mr. Wodehouse is not an emigré in the same sense as these Central European writers are. But since the outbreak of World War I his permanent home has been outside these islands and he is cherishing the memory of an old and very dead world. Gallantly he strives to keep it alive. When the Turks were besieging a Central European fortress in the 16th century, the Sultan, Suleiman II, died. His death, had it become generally known, would have been a blow to the morale of his armies. So the dead Sultan was placed on his throne and after the siege, the victorious Turks marched past, saluting the corpse. Mr. Wodehouse's *oeuvre* is also a march past in salute of a corpse. His books written in the last 38 years are obituary notices on the Edwardian era: untrue and eulogistic—as most decent obituary notices are expected to be. Yes, eulogistic, because in spite of the apparent or, maybe, intended, caricature, the Wodehouse-world is a cheerful, carefree, sunny, debonair and hilarious world.

He never makes jokes on serious subjects. Nothing is stranger to his mentality than Swift's morbid and immortal joke, the *Modest Proposal*. Mr. Wodehouse would never advise hungry mothers in time of famine to consume their offspring with a tasty sauce. In time of famine, great fires and plagues Wodehouse would go on writing about

Ukridge, Bertie Wooster and Jeeves, as he did in two great
wars, even when he was an internee in the last one. Every
now and then you can find in his novels a faint allusion
to political matters. Psmith called himself a Socialist.
Mr. Wodehouse admired Mussolini—but not as a Fascist
(he never understood the nature of Fascism) but as a
"strong man". Cedric Mulliner had a terrifying and
forbidding secretary whom he wished to dismiss but
never dared to. "Mussolini might have fired her, if at
the top of his form, but I can think of nobody else
capable of the feat." Even the beloved Jeeves is once
described as "a domestic Mussolini". Hitler—according to
the best of my knowledge—is not mentioned at all, favour-
ably or otherwise, although he was as strong a man as
Mussolini, to put it no higher. Russia is not liked by Mr.
Wodehouse. "This police persecution must stop . . . We are
not in Russia." There are other references to Soviet Russia in
several books, always unfavourable but never going beyond
the scope of music-hall jokes. Stalin ranks with Al Capone.
In *Thank You Jeeves*, Wooster's new valet, Brinkley, wants
to kill Bertie and some other heroes of the novel with a
carving knife. Later Jeeves enquires whether Bertie intends
to retain Brinkley. This is Bertie's answer: "Retain him
in my employment? After finishing first by the shortest of
heads in the race with him and his carving knife? I do not
so intend, Jeeves. Stalin, yes. Al Capone, certainly. But not
Brinkley." The great war (No. II) itself was a major but
regrettable falling out between respectable gentlemen. Mr.
Wodehouse published an article in the *Saturday Evening
Post*, written in German internment:

"I never was interested," (it read) "in politics. I'm quite
unable to work up any kind of belligerent feeling. Just as
I'm about to feel belligerent about some country I meet
a decent sort of chap. We go out together and lose any
fighting thoughts or feelings."

It was as simple as that. He would not have said all that

about the Russians but he said it about the Germans—after the fall of France. Subsequently, some people tried to read Fascist tendencies into his earlier writings. But this is nonsense. Wodehouse is not a Fascist: he does not even understand Fascism. You do not need to be brilliantly intelligent to understand the nature of Fascism but Wodehouse lacks that kind of intelligence. He is an able and ingenious comic writer; but he is not an intelligent man. The second reason for having spoken as he did is his genuine good nature. He cannot be spiteful; he has no hatred in his heart. He refuses to notice any ugliness in this world. If a certain kind of ugliness is too conspicuous, he looks away; if it is too near— he goes away. He is the escapist, who actually does escape. Thus the Nazis, too, were good beans and soundish sorts of crumpets. Most of the characters of his light-comedy novels (as opposed to the farcical ones) are noble and self-sacrificing. In *Something Fresh*, for example, Joan refuses to accept half of the £1000 fee promised for a certain job, unless she is allowed to deserve it by doing her bit; but Ashe wants her to take that sum for no service at all. Aline, the daughter of an American millionaire, deprives herself of all decent food for months, because her father is on a diet and to see others eat would cause him pain, etc., etc. All these Wodehouse-characters are gentle and noble souls, or, at least they are "playing the game". Even the peppery, quarrelsome American millionaire is transformed into a fairy god-father at the end of the story mentioned, because the goodness of the others had melted his heart. So why not melt Hitler's heart? Or Himmler's? The Russians, of course, are a different kind of bird, for the simple reason that they wish to destroy Bertie Wooster's world and expropriate Blandings Castle. That is unforgivable. Unless Malenkov puts out all suchlike ideas from his head, he won't even be regarded as a candidate for the Drones Club.

Sex is out, too—not only politics. George Orwell writes: "How closely Wodehouse sticks to the conventional morality can be seen from the fact that nowhere in his books is there anything in the nature of a sex joke. This is an enormous sacrifice for a farcical writer to make." I do not think it was an "enormous sacrifice". It just happens that Wodehouse's morality is conventional and sex is something unclean for him—not to be touched upon. He is not self-sacrificing; he is suburban. Of course, people fall in love, they may even kiss each other in the garden, but once they have kissed, they will almost certainly have to be united in holy matrimony. A beautiful or charming girl inspires only one thought in a Wodehouse hero's mind: the thought of marriage. Pauline Stoker did spend a night in Bertie Wooster's cottage and her father took rather a poor view of this—but the reader knows that Bertie himself moved out to sleep in the coal shed and did not even think of the possibilities which seem to have crossed Mr. Stoker's as well as the reader's mind. Wodehouse is clean; life is a shade dirtier. And he is content to be one of the few humorists who do not wish to be taken seriously.

The problems his heroes have to face are not world-shaking or metaphysical problems. How to get a snake out of a fellow-guest's bed in a country house? How to get out of a taxi without it being noticed that you are wearing yellow shoes with a morning coat? How to get boot polish off your face? Should you, or should you not, imitate, in certain circumstances, a hen laying an egg? Mr. Wodehouse is under no delusion. He is fully aware of the fact that these are minor problems.

He makes such wanton use of coincidence, that he cannot possibly expect anyone to accept these occurrences as likely. I have just referred to *Something Fresh*, so we might as well stick to that novel for another set of examples. The Hon. Freddie Threepwood, the Earl of Emsworth's son, is engaged to Aline, the daughter of an American millionaire but they do not love each other truly and fondly. It is George Emerson who loves Aline with the proper intensity and, oddly enough, Freddie, the fiancé, and George, his rival—unknown to each other—happen to get acquainted at a boxing match and Freddie invites George to Blandings Castle for the week-end. There is a girl who is in possession of some compromising letters written by Freddie and she turns out to be the other hero's, Ashe Marson's, beloved Joan. It also turns out that Aline and Joan had been at school together. R. Jones the crook goes to visit Joan to have a word with her about Freddie's letters and he happens to meet Aline in the house and happens to be able to eaves-drop on an important conversation between the two girls. Aline and Joan decide that the latter should go down to Blandings Castle disguised as the former's parlour-maid. But if Joan is a disguised parlour-maid, her boy-friend, Ashe, must be a disguised valet, at the same place and at the same time. How is this achieved? Well, Ashe is looking for a job and he happens to get one as the private secretary of Aline's father and he has to be disguised as a valet and—needless to say—has to accompany him to Blandings Castle. And so on, and so on. There are many similar occurrences in the same story. This would be all right in a purely farcical novel. But *Something Fresh* is light comedy and the reader is supposed to take some interest in the story. I am sure many readers do; I personally found it excruciatingly boring.

All Wodehouse books are permeated by an air of perverted snobbishness. Mr. Wodehouse is supposed to be a critic, or at least, a caricaturist of the upper classes but, in fact, he is their sycophant, just like the gossip-writers in the evening papers. It has been repeatedly said of Mr. Wode-house that there is no development in his art. There is no artistic development but there are different grades of snob-bishness. He started with school-stories and even this early period saw some changes in him. "Wrykyn, Wodehouse's imaginary public school," (writes George Orwell) "is a school of a more fashionable type than Dulwich and one gets the impression that between *The Gold Bat* (1904) and *Mike* (1909) Wrykyn itself has become more expensive and moved farther from London." As success came and Mr. Wodehouse moved up higher and higher on the social and income-ladder, so also did his heroes ascend. Psmith and Ukridge—the latter always broke and always just about to make a colossal fortune—were followed by the Earl of Emsworth and the Blandings Castle set. Wooster and Jeeves came later. Bertram Wooster is no aristocrat, but many of his friends are. Cricket and football, too, were replaced by golf in the later stories and the ordinary pub-crawlers, suburban dwellers and people of common stock were gradually purged and liquidated—with the exception of Ukridge, whom Wodehouse liked very much and who died hard. The American period is another distinct phase. At that time Mr. Wodehouse tried to please readers on both sides, and there were American characters in his novels set in England and English characters in novels set in America. In the last period he mostly produced novels on the light-comedy line. The titled personages still crowd each other out on every page.

Mr. Wodehouse lost the British Public's affection and admiration during the war—although, I believe, he deserved neither the former adulation, nor the subsequent fall from grace. I shall have more to say about these war-time events a little later. Here I only wish to remark that Wodehouses's tragedy—if tragedy it was—is a very human story, more human than anything to be found in his books. He was loved as a satirist although he was a simple idoliser. Later, he fell from grace because of a crime he did not mean to commit. In other words: he was hailed as something he never was and was eventually cold-shouldered for a crime he never committed. Finally, the British Public—after a grave error in judgment committed by Wodehouse during the war—did not turn against him as a bad patriot; they simply dropped him as a writer. He had to be interviewed on the Nazi radio for the British Public to discover—not that he was not a patriotic Englishman—but that he was not half as funny as they had thought. His books still appear with unfailing regularity; they are still read by many and probably have large sales. But Mr. Wodehouse is no longer news; he is not really interesting. He is not a writer; he is a habit. It must be added—in defence of British taste—that although Mr. Wodehouse still writes in the same vein as before, he does not write so well.

Returning to the various phases of his career, I must add they are not quite clearly defined. His childish snobbishness, however, is always there and always irritating. He accepts the position of "our betters" in society. Jeeves is a feudal figure—one of his greatest virtues being his fidelity to his employer. Valets, butlers, parlour-maids and club-stewards are the only workers he can describe with any accuracy—and the only ones he is interested in. Sharp class distinction is always drawn—with a superior smile—even between the servants. In Blandings Castle there is a complicated order of privilege from the butler down to the odd-job man, through valets, footmen, lady's maids, parlour-maids, house-maids, laundry-maids and others. Some of them have their meals in the Steward's room, others in the Servants' Hall and others again in the house-maids' sitting room. (This last and lowest place is even deprived of its capital letters.) It is a delicious episode, when Slingsby, the chauffeur, is being promoted socially from the Servants' Hall to the Steward's room.

None of his major and famous figures follow any occupation. Archie Moffam is out to get a job in New York ("The general scheme was that I should kind of look round, you know, and nose about and buzz to and fro till something turned up. That was, broadly speaking, the notion."); Bertie Wooster is a gentleman of means; Ukridge has many temporary schemes but no job or profession; Lord Emsworth is a lord by trade; and although Psmith works at one time in the City the author is at pains to emphasise that he does not really need to work. Real gentlemen just do not work. Mr. Hayward describes the Drones Club in these approving words: "The 'drone', a type of good-natured, irresponsible young man-about-town . . . is common to almost all Mr. Wodehouse's novels and short stories." Are drones and parasites really quite as charming as that? Beggars, too, may be drones, but as they usually belong to a lower social order, they are treated more harshly by Mr. Wodehouse: ". . . beggars approached the task of trying to persuade perfect strangers to bear the burden of their main-tenance." Those who have no money and no fellow-para-sites to borrow from—are hardly better than criminals. The "Wanted" column of the morning paper is a sort of dredger "which churns up strange creatures from the mud of London's under-world". Apparently those who are after a job.

Among Mr. Wodehouse's better known heroes, only Jeeves has a proper calling and he is a valet. All the other silly young men were at Eton (or some inferior school like Harrow) and Oxford. Even a minor hero like Ashe Marson is not allowed to escape without a degree. He "managed to obtain a sort of degree, enough to enable him to call himself a Bachelor of Arts." About Ashe, Orwell remarks: "The hero of *Something Fresh* (1915) escapes from low-class journalism by becoming physical training instructor to a dyspeptic millionaire: this is regarded as a step up, morally as well as financially." It is true that all these upper class heroes are extremely silly. But no decent Englishman of the Edwardian era (that means, no Englishman with an accept-able and preferably unearned income) aspired to being intelligent. To be "clever" was bad form. Indeed, only Jeeves is supposed to be clever; and he is the most dishonest of all Wodehouse's characters. Cleverness and dishonesty go hand in hand. And anyway, cleverness, if needed at all, can always be hired for a small weekly sum, in the person of a gentleman's gentleman.

Most of Mr. Wodehouse's characters are simple and stereotyped figures. Sometimes the humour is based on psychological observations and such attempts, though rare, are usually very successful. The American millionaire is a man of boundless energy, so when he takes up collecting scarabs—to take his mind off his business—he throws himself into his new hobby with his customary ferocious and passionate zeal. He collects scarabs as he used to collect dollars—frantically and mercilessly. Ashe Marson easily gains the upper hand over his ill-tempered and aggressive millionaire, but shrinks to nothingness in the presence of the august butler, Beach. Or again the two golfers are forced to compete for the hand of a girl whom they both loathe. The winner of the game is to have the girl, so they are both trying to lose. But through sheer good—or bad—luck, they both start off magnificently, and after that both throw themselves into the the game with zeal and are determined to have one really good score in their lives—and never mind the girl!

Some of the types which populate the books are funny, others again are not so funny. He has never been able to create a loveable female character, although he has attempted many. All these girls have hearts of gold, the author waxes sentimental over them—a pitfall for many humorists—and the general effect is that they are too good to be true, or even to be amusing. It is interesting to note, that although Mr. Wodehouse is always sentimental about love, he is never sentimental about orphans, widows, lonely women or children. Indeed, the usual child he describes is a revolting and repulsive little brute, bearing some such name as Old Stinker. Parents compete in his stories as to whose child is the uglier and the child's only role in the Wodehouse story is to be a perfect nuisance. ("Something that will be a help to them [two children] in their after lives

[one of his heroes muses]. Not that I care a damn about
their after lives, except that I hope they'll all choke.")

The types he describes are one-dimensional. Mr. Wickham is the aesthetic brute; Emsworth's private secretary is
efficient; Joan is the independent, modern girl—a faint and
non-political echo of the suffragettes; R. Jones is the crook;
George Emerson is the determined young man; Peters is
the querulous millionaire; Roberta Wickham the "*enfant
terrible*" of the twenties. All Wodehouse butlers are the
stereotyped stage-butlers. "Bowles (he writes in Ukridge)
was an ex-butler, and about him, as about all ex-butlers,
there clung like a garment an aura of dignified superiority
which had never failed to crush my spirit." Americans
mostly belong to two groups: they are either millionaires—
energetic and rude and dragging daughters about—or film-
stars, mad on crazy publicity stunts.

But Mr. Wodehouse's happiest creations are the idiots.
He is at his best in their portrayal. His favourite kind of
stupidity is the Mayfair and Drones Club sort of woolly-
headedness, coupled with almost complete illiteracy. ("And
what, Archibald asked himself, could he do? Absolutely
nothing, except give an imitation of a hen laying an egg.")
His range in idiots is large, his selection varied. The Earl
of Emsworth is an absent-minded idiot; his son, Freddie
Threepwood is an idiot who makes a fool of himself
vis-à-vis chorus girls and who dreads his father; Ukridge is
an idiotic dreamer about large fortunes to be made; Bertie
Wooster is an idiot who is always trying to smooth matters
out but muddles everything up so that he, himself, is regarded for a short time by the friend he wanted to help as
the villain of the piece; Archie is a brave idiot; Osbert
Mulliner a cowardly idiot. The list could be continued almost indefinitely. All these people are alive; they are funny;
they are the best he ever created. Not forgetting Jeeves, of
course, who is not exactly a wizard or a sage—but in this
company his mental powers excel. Mr. Wodehouse is on

happy ground when he succeeds in finding someone who is even more stupid than his average hero. Battling Billson, the boxer, formerly of the Merchant Marine, is one of these happy discoveries. He has a heart of gold and when he learns that his opponent is in trouble or was "up all night looking after his wife who had burned her finger at the jam factory"—his golden heart melts and he lets the other fellow win. Billson is funny; his intelligence is also just a little above that of an average gorilla. Mr. Wodehouse is the bard of stupidity. One wonders if he could draw a really sophisticated character. He never tried.

In all his novels everything always ends well. But these happy endings make you wonder. It is an essential part of a happy ending that the Hon. Freddie Threepwood has his allowance restored and has, once again, sufficient means to squander on chorus girls, drink, and his chums. Or take the *Indiscretions of Archie*. Archie Moffam marries the daughter of an American hotel-millionaire who hates Archie warmly. Archie, the drone, is supposed to be the sympathetic character and his father-in-law—who is not disarmed by Archie's "good family" and public school manners—is a villain. (Only a Wodehouse-villain, of course —so not devilishly villainous.) In the end, however, everything is made up and forgiven, when Archie breaks the news that his wife is going to have a baby. This is the best knews the fierce father-in-law has ever heard in his life. Happy and delighted, he embraces Archie. (Why he ever doubted Archie's powers of reproduction, is not quite clear.)

I think Mr. Wodehouse's writings have a demoralising effect. He is not intentionally immoral, indeed, nothing could be more noble and praiseworthy than his intentions and his consciously accepted moral code. But although he acclimatised himself in the county-house and Blandings-castle world, his moral outlook remained suburban. And the suburban code—like many rigidly conventional codes— is often immoral. Wodehouse has great admiration for money and birth, for the good-for-nothing and the drone (he is always on their side—not one of them ever received the dire punishment of being compelled to do some proper work); he idolises stupidity; and—in spite of his best intentions and because of his genuine good heart he draws a false picture of the world around us. His caricature does not emphasise the big nose; it retouches the warts. Many readers will say that these are harsh, unjust, indeed, pompous words about a kind and modest writer who does not even pretend to be more than a "mere entertainer". (Why "mere"? Is it so easy to entertain?) But every writer—comic or tragic, small or great—has a message; or at least pictures a certain kind of life, accepts certain values and rejects others. A successful author with Wodehouse's vast following cannot be dismissed as insignificant. But he is an engaging character at the same time. Patient, well-meaning, good-hearted and utterly lacking in venom and gall. He hates quarrels. He is an escapist but not a cowardly escapist; he simply dislikes the disagreeable and ugly.

Pelham Granville Wodehouse is 74 years old. He was born at Guildford, of middle-class parents, and educated in Dulwich College. For two years he worked as a clerk in a London bank. In 1903 he started a column *By the Way* in the *Globe*, and was soon able to support himself as a contributor to comic papers and later as a novelist. He visited the United States in 1904. "After returning to London from his first American trip, he went to the country and buried himself in an almost empty house with no company but that of twelve dogs."* In 1914, he married a widow, Mrs. Ethel Rowley. After the outbreak of World War I he crossed the Atlantic and made America his more or less permanent home. Between 1910 and 1940 he published about two new books every year. In 1940 he was living in Le Touquet and was captured by the Germans. After the end of the war he returned to the United States.

* 20th Century Authors.

From the various short biographies in works of reference we may learn that "he is completely bald, shy and utterly unpractical". This latter statement means that "his wife handles all their money".

On two occasions in Mr. Wodehouse's life, his name appeared in the news columns of the papers instead of on the literary page. The first was in June, 1939, when he was made an honorary Doctor of Literature at Oxford. The *Times* said that the Public Orator "paid tribute to the kindly temper and finished style of Mr. Wodehouse's work but also achieved the difficult task of presenting or suggesting in Latin the familiar figures of Bertie Wooster and Jeeves and Mr. Mulliner and Lord Emsworth and the Empress of Blandings and Psmith and even the Honourable Augustus Fink-Nottle and the love life of the newts." The Vice-Chancellor admitted Mr. Wodehouse with the words: "*Vir lepidissime, facetissime, venustissime, jocosissime, ridibundissime, te cum turba tua Leporum Facitiarum Venustatum Iocurum Risuum, ego auctoritate mea et totius Universitatis admitto ad graduum Doctoris in Litteris honoris causa.*"

The second occasion, when Mr. Wodehouse became news was in 1941. When the Germans captured him, they first kept him under surveillance in Le Touquet but he was later removed to Germany for internment. There, he said in June, 1941, to interviewing journalists, he had learnt to sew, darn, sole shoes and wash shirts. All this, in itself, would have caused only a minor sensation. In June, 1941, however, the Berlin correspondent of a Swedish newspaper reported that Mr. P. G. Wodehouse had been set free from an internment camp near Breslau and was staying in the Adlon Hotel, Berlin. (The report added that Mr. Wodehouse had finished one book and was finishing another— about Blandings Castle.) Following this report, another message told us that Mr. Wodehouse was to broadcast on his own experiences on the German radio once a week.

The talks—he was reported to have said—"would be general chats, entirely non-political".

This news created an uproar in Britain. The Germans explained: "Mr. Wodehouse reached the age of 60 last October and was automatically released." To be exact, it was in October, 1941, that Mr. Wodehouse reached the age of 60. Nor did the "automatic release" story explain why Mr. Wodehouse was being interviewed on the Nazi radio. He was bitterly attacked in this country. There came a point, however, when the attack over-reached itself. "Cassandra" of the *Daily Mirror* delivered an hysterical philippic against Wodehouse in a B.B.C. "postscript". He freely used the word "quisling" and said things like this: " . . . his last and greatest sale—that of his own country." This preposterous attack won back a great deal of sympathy for Mr. Wodehouse. Many people decided that it would be wise to suspend judgment and hear what Wodehouse had to say about all this. He was far from forgiven —that was impossible at the time—and even the moderate Mr. Eden declared in the House of Commons in July, 1941: "His Majesty's Government have seen with regret the report that Mr. Wodehouse has lent his services to the German propaganda machine." At the end of the war— although the *affaire Wodehouse* was not forgotten—there was no outcry for a trial. Mr. Wodehouse, I firmly believe, committed no worse crime than that of stupidity.

What was in his mind? English gentlemen were quarrelling with German gentlemen and it was the plain duty of all decent eggs and soundish beans to try to bring them nearer to one another. "Dismiss the whole thing from your mind. Might have happened to anybody. Faults on both sides and so forth." Oh, yes, he may have realised that to broadcast Nazi propaganda on the German radio was wrong; but why not give funny talks, pure humour and lighthearted chit-chat? The fact that all this happened at the time of Germany's attack on Russia might, it is true, suggest that the matter was not quite as innocent as that. But there can be little doubt that it was. At the time of the attack on Russia, Mr. Wodehouse had already agreed to give his talks. "Why am I going to broadcast for the Germans? Well, they asked me, that's all."

"In making the proposal Plack (Goebbels' assistant) showed that he knew his man. He knew that Wodehouse made fun of the English in all his stories and that he seldom wrote in any other way, that he was still living in the period about which he wrote and had no conception of Nazism and all it meant. Wodehouse was his own Bertie Wooster."*

I believe—as I have tried to show—that Wodehouse never made fun of the English in the sense Flannery and Goebbels believed he had. The simple truth is that Mr. Wodehouse was not "his own" Bertie Wooster. He was and is identical with Bertie Wooster and that's all there is to it. His tragedy was that Jeeves was not interned with him. Surely, we are not going to hold that against him?

* *Assignment to Berlin*, by Harry W. Flannery, Michael Joseph, 1942

BIBLIOGRAPHY

The Pothunters, 1902
A Prefect's Uncle, 1903
A Good Bet, 1904
The Head of Kay's, 1905
Love Among the Chickens, 1906
The White Feather, 1907
The Swoop, 1908
Mike, 1909
Enter Psmith, 1909
A Gentleman of Leisure, 1910
Psmith in the City, 1910
The Prince and Betty, 1911
The Little Nugget, 1912

Psmith: the Journalist, 1915
Something Fresh, 1915
Uneasy Money, 1917
Piccadilly Jim, 1918
A Damsel in Distress, 1919
Jill, the Reckless, 1920
The Coming of Bill, 1920
The Indiscretions of Archie, 1921
The Clicking of Cuthbert, 1922
The Girl on the Boat, 1922
Mostly Sally, 1923
Leave it to Psmith, 1923
Bill the Conqueror, 1924
The Inimitable Jeeves, 1924
Ukridge, 1924
Carry on, Jeeves, 1925
Sam the Sudden, 1925
Sam in the Suburbs, 1925
The Heart of a Goof, 1926
Meet Mr. Mulliner, 1927
The Small Bachelor, 1927
Money for Nothing, 1928
Fight Preferred, 1929
Summer Lightning, 1929
Baa Baa, Black Sheep (play with Ian Hay) 1930
Very Good, Jeeves, 1930
Big Money, 1931
If I were You, 1931
Hot Water, 1932
Louder and Funnier, 1932
Dr. Sally, 1932
Heavy Weather, 1933
Mulliner Nights, 1933
Right-Ho, Jeeves, 1934
Candle Light (play), 1934
Thank You, Jeeves, 1934

Blandings Castle, 1935
The Luck of the Bodkins, 1935
The Inside Stand (play), 1935
Laughing Gas, 1936
Young Men in Spats, 1936
The Crime Wave at Blandings, 1937
Lord Emsworth, 1937
The Code of the Woosters, 1938
Summer Moonshine, 1938
Uncle Fred in the Springtime, 1939
Divots, 1939
Quick Service, 1940
Eggs, Beans and Crumpets, 1940
Money in the Bank, 1942
Full Moon, 1947
Uncle Dynamite, 1948
Mating Season, 1949
Nothing Serious, 1950
The Old Reliable, 1951
Barmy in Wonderland, 1952
Pigs Have Wings, 1952
Performing Flea (Foreword and notes by W. Townend)
  1953